ROUTLEDGE LIBRARY E
PHILOSOPHY OF REL

HEAVEN WASN'T HIS DESTINATION

HEAVEN WASN'T HIS DESTINATION
The Philosophy of Ludwig Feuerbach

WILLIAM B. CHAMBERLAIN

Volume 7

Routledge
Taylor & Francis Group
LONDON AND NEW YORK

First published 1941 by Routledge

2 Park Square, Milton Park, Abingdon, Oxon OX14 4RN
711 Third Avenue, New York, NY 10017, USA

Routledge is an imprint of the Taylor & Francis Group, an informa business

First issued in paperback 2016

British Library Cataloguing in Publication Data
A catalogue record for this book is available from the British Library

ISBN 978-1-138-99216-0 (pbk)
ISBN 978-0-415-82224-4 (hbk)
ISBN 978-0-203-53351-2 (ebk)

Publisher's Note
The publisher has gone to great lengths to ensure the quality of this reprint but
points out that some imperfections in the original copies may be apparent.

Disclaimer
The publisher has made every effort to trace copyright holders and would
welcome correspondence from those they have been unable to trace.

HEAVEN
WASN'T
HIS
DESTINATION

The Philosophy
of
Ludwig Feuerbach

by

William B.
Chamberlain

London
George Allen and Unwin Ltd

FIRST PUBLISHED IN 1941

PRINTED IN GREAT BRITAIN
in 11-Point Fournier Type
BY UNWIN BROTHERS LIMITED
WOKING

To
FREDERIC
and
LYDIA

"Man is the measure of all things"

PROTAGORAS

"I am the philosopher of the
common man"

FEUERBACH

Preface

The philosophy of Feuerbach has received very little direct treatment in the English language. Engels' *Ludwig Feuerbach* has been translated and rather generally read, but this brochure takes Feuerbach as a jumping-off place, rather than concerning itself directly with him. Dr. Sidney Hook's *From Hegel to Marx* devotes two excellent chapters to Feuerbach in which the latter's conclusions are summarized, but in no sense exhaustively discussed. As the title indicates, Dr. Hook's chief interest is considerably wider than the philosophy of Feuerbach. Aside from these two books, there exists virtually nothing on Feuerbach in English.

In French there is Lévy's *La Philosophie de Feuerbach*, a highly comprehensive work, though criticized by Marxists as too Feuerbachian; and in Germany there is, of course, a rather more considerable literature in which the works of Starcke, Bolin, Rawidowicz, and others on the technical side are complemented by the Marxist writings on the broader, historical side. Most of these are noted in the bibliography at the end of the book.

In quoting Feuerbach I have, in general, taken such English translations as are available, i.e. that of George Eliot—upon which one could scarcely expect to improve—in *The Essence of Christianity*, and some excerpts from Dr. Hook, who is as able a translator as he is a philosopher. The rest of the translations, for which I herewith wish to make apology, are my own; although I have occasionally, as noted, taken advantage of the help of the French transla-

tions of Lévy and Roy in order to shake myself free of the
—to me, at least—often cumbrous and difficult German
philosophical idiom. Especially, furthermore, must I plead
guilty to the attempt to render into scarcely lyric English
verse the quoted lines of the poets Herwegh and Keller.

Only rarely do I intersperse non-English words throughout the text, for, in my judgment, there are already too many
commentaries and supposed translations which leave
numerous crucial expressions in the original. Such readers
as can well understand the latter can read, and often have,
read the original texts throughout and do not need this
linguistic by-play. To those who do not read the original,
it cannot make much difference, anyway.

It is my agreeable task here to express my appreciation
to three outstanding philosophical minds who have, both
directly and collaterally, aided me in the clarification of my
thought: Dr. Marvin Farber of the University of Buffalo,
U.S.A., and the eminent Professors Charles Werner and
Henri Reverdin of the University of Geneva, to which
institution this book was first presented as a doctoral disser-
tation. I also wish especially to express my appreciation to
Mr. Francis A. Henson who, though seeing far beyond me,
has been my friend and guide in my wanderings through
what I used to consider the maze of religion and radicalism;
and to Rev. Herman J. Hahn, a socialist Christian who, in
his every word and action, demonstrates the vital truth of
the fundamental attitude expressed on these pages. None of
these, need I add, is directly responsible for anything said
in this book. What I have said that will be deemed bad is
despite them; what I have said that by history will be proven
good, is because of them.

To my wife I wish to try to express a gratitude inexpressible: for her stenographic and editorial help, for her indispensable criticism, and for her unflagging encouragement and inspiration.

And, lastly, I wish to express my respect for magistral pillars, millions of books, an ever-efficient personnel to whom, immersed in a great and beloved concretization of "history," one war does not seem to be very important—the British Museum. In its high-domed reading-room have read and written some of the greatest spirits of our era, among them one who, taking some of the insights discussed in this book, welded them into a philosophy which has shaken the world and in the light of which all future philosophies will have to be judged.

To that distinguished company I belonged while reading and writing there.

W. B. C.

LONDON

November 1939

Contents

INTRODUCTION

The object of this book is twofold. It is its intention to pay humble tribute to a little-understood philosopher whose stature grows with the years, and in so doing perhaps to provide a key to the question of religion and personal immortality for those who reject philosophical idealism and a personal God—in short, are philosophical materialists—but who feel lumps in their throats when reading the exhortation to Deity at the end of Thomas Mann's historic letter to the rector of the University of Bonn, and do not know why. Many knew why when a book called *The Essence of Christianity* was published a century ago. But now a century's dust lies on those pages, and few are those who will brush it off to read. And fewer still who will record their dusting in the English language.

Many of Ludwig Feuerbach's disciples are better known to history than is their modest master. Among them figure world-famous poets, politicians, dramatists, and composers. But in his own day he had many a celebrator, many a vilifier. Of him his contemporary, David Strauss, wrote: "To-day, and perhaps for some time to come, the field belongs to him. His theory is the truth for this age."[1] Another of his contemporaries, an English divine, said that

---

[1] Strauss, *Ausgewählte Briefe*, Bonn, 1874, p. 184.

15

Feuerbach ought to be annihilated. "Aye, annihilate; for this is not a matter in which we pretend to one morsel of tolerance."[1] This invective even extended to Feuerbach's English translator, Marian Evans, better known to literary history under her pen name, "George Eliot." Of her the same reverend gentleman says, "There is an impudicity of the mind more loathsome than any impudicity of the body, and Magdalene asylums may be needed for others besides the unfortunate beings who seek a refuge from guilt and misery there!"[2]

Another Englishman, on the other hand, has this to say of Feuerbach: "I confess that to Feuerbach I owe a debt of inestimable gratitude. Feeling about in uncertainty for the ground, and finding everywhere shifting sands, Feuerbach cast a sudden blaze into the darkness, and disclosed to me the way."[3] And the international Engels, speaking about the publication of *The Essence of Christianity*, says: "One must himself have experienced the liberating effect of this book to get an idea of it. Enthusiasm was general; we all became at once Feuerbachians."[4]

If forced to state Feuerbach's philosophical genealogy, one would have to say that he was son of Hegel and father to Marx.* While this is true, it is too gross a simplification to give proper credit to the son and grandson. Feuerbach was as extraordinary a son as was Marx a grandson. For he

---

[1] William Maccall, review of *Das Wesen des Christenthums*, written in 1854, published in *The Newest Materialism*, London, 1873, p. 117.

[2] Ibid., p. 120.

[3] S. Baring-Gould, *The Origin and Development of Religious Belief*, Part II, Preface, p. xii.

[4] Engels, *Ludwig Feuerbach*, 2nd English ed., London, 1935, p. 28.

* Comte was, as we shall see later, his half-brother.

saw far beyond most of the Young Hegelians, and brought to the solution of problems inevitably perplexing to Hegelians a new approach which, to continue the metaphor, was not in the Hegelian genes. Just as Marx, in turn, adduced important elements decidedly not in the family blood. While it is certain that the welding of natural science materialism and the Hegelian dialectic into the system of historical materialism was chiefly effected by Marx and Engels, it is also increasingly obvious that the Young Hegelians—and especially Feuerbach—played a considerable role, not only in laying the groundwork, but also in unconsciously establishing certain parts of the structure of dialectical materialism. To what extent this is true will be examined in this book.

At first glance it might seem that those who are interested in the social and political, rather than the philosophical, aspects of the problems raised by the transition from Hegelian idealism to historical materialism would have nothing to learn from Feuerbach, who occupied himself relatively little with politics and was almost exclusively interested in the question of religion, Christianity, and immortality. It is important to realize, however, that many of the most important battles leading up to the revolution of 1848 in Germany were fought with philosophical, and even theological, weapons. This was due firstly to the fact that liberty of political utterance was at that time decidedly restricted in the German states; and secondly to the fact that philosophical polemics were close to the heart and mind of almost all of the educated population,* save per-

* cf. Lange: "The efforts for the unity of the Fatherland might for a season be forgotten, but not those for the unity of the reason. . . . Ger-

haps the ruling class which had appointed Hegel its official mind. Thus the rest of the populace could carry on the struggle in appropriate cosmological and ontological terms without interference from above. Also, be it added, if politics are defined as the science of aggregate existence in the world, and philosophy as the art of explaining existence and the world, the rapports between these two are obviously closer than they generally seem to be. In any case, these rapports were clearer in nineteenth-century Germany than they are in twentieth-century anyplace.*

Another reason for serious consideration of the philosophy of Feuerbach is the light which it sheds upon the general problem of historical materialism and Christianity. True, Feuerbach never mentions dialectics, and he considers the individual aspects of religious experience rather than the social aspects of religion. But he throws out important suggestions, some of which, when tracked down, will provide fundamental material for the serious work on dialectical materialism and Christianity for which the world has been waiting, and which—be it hastily added—this book is not.

Feuerbach was not a revolutionary in the sense in which Marx and Engels were revolutionaries. The latter tried to bring him into the communist movement in 1845. In a letter to Marx dated February 22nd of that year, Engels wrote: "Feuerbach says that he must finish his extended

many is the only country in the world where the apothecary cannot make up a prescription without being conscious of the relation of his activity to the constitution of the universe."—*History of Materialism*, 3rd ed., London, 1925, Book II, p. 263.

* The Russia of the Bolsheviks might be excepted. Discussion of this point would, however, lead us afield at the moment.

criticism of religion before being able to concern himself sufficiently with communism to be capable of defending it in his writing. He adds that in Bavaria he is too isolated from life to keep informed as to what is going on in the world. Aside from that, he is a communist; it is for him only a question of knowing methods for carrying on. If it is possible for him, he will come to the Rhine this summer, and afterwards he may go to Brussels. We will let him know what he should do."[1] But Engels' hope was in vain. Feuerbach emerged neither from his Bavarian solitude nor from his preoccupation with the religious question, though he did pay dues to Marx's party, and was considered a leader among the "true socialists," Grün, Moses Hess, and their school.

What, then, was Feuerbach's contribution? And why should we concern ourselves with him?

The answer can be simply stated. Feuerbach's contribution was in his writings on religion and philosophy, each of them a manifesto to humanity, telling us that the desires of men can be satisfied here below.

[1] Mehring, *Nachlass von Marx, Engels, Lassalle*, vol. ii, p. 347.

Chapter I

IDEALISM AND POSITIVISM

An uncrowned monarch was ruler of German thought in 1824. In that year there came to the capital a young ex-student of theology, one of the ruler's subjects. The young subject was not long a subject; he rebelled against the monarch's Absolute, and he went away. No one expected to hear more of him. Two decades later the monarch was dead; the court was divided and dispersed; and the rebellious ex-subject was acknowledged arch-rebel of the day; "the whole of German philosophy and culture stood within his shadow."[1] The monarch was Hegel; his rebel subject was Feuerbach.

The fourth of the five sons of the eminent criminal lawyer and jurist, Ritter Anselm von Feuerbach, was born in Landshut in Bavaria July 28, 1804.[2] His name was Ludwig Andreas. During Ludwig's boyhood his father's career led the family from Landshut to Munich; thence to Bamberg, and thence to Ansbach, where Ludwig finished his studies in the Gymnasium in 1822. In the following

---

[1] Sidney Hook, *From Hegel to Marx*, London, 1936, p. 220.
[2] Biographical data taken from C. Beyer, *Leben und Geist Ludwig Feuerbachs*, Leipzig, 1873; and preface to C. N. Starcke's *Ludwig Feuerbach*, Stuttgart, 1885.

year he matriculated at Heidelberg, intending to pursue theological studies. But he was uninspired by his teachers, save Professor Daub, and found that his bent was rather for philosophy than theology. He therefore went to Berlin, "led by the call of Hegel"[1] and pushed by the hand of Daub. His discipleship there lasted two years. He was a good student, but his discontent and disagreement with much of Hegel's system, as well as the drive of his inchoate humanism, prevented him from absorbing as much as he might otherwise have absorbed at the fount of Hegelian wisdom.

Feuerbach concluded his academic career at Erlangen, studying philosophy and natural science. It was there that he wrote his unorthodox *Gedanken uber Tod und Unsterblichkeit* ("Thoughts on Death and Immortality"),* anonymously published in 1830. The fact of his authorship, however, soon leaked out, and he was branded as a radical. This fact, coupled with Feuerbach's awkward and embarrassed manner of public delivery, precluded the possibility of a professional career for him, although he did work for a few years as an unsalaried *docent* at Erlangen. During the 1830s Feuerbach lived precariously, struggling for a hand-to-mouth living, and writing. In 1833 and 1837, respectively, he published his two volumes, *Die Geschichte des Neueren Philosophie* ("The History of the Newer Philosophy"). And between these, in 1834, he wrote his

---

[1] Starcke, loc. cit., p. xi.

* As Feuerbach's works are first mentioned in this chapter, the German titles of them will be given, with the English equivalents in parentheses. These references once established, further mention of them will uniformly be in English.

Abälard und Heloise. In 1837 he married Bertha Low and moved to Bruckberg, where was located the porcelain factory which was to provide him a modest living until 1860. A share in the factory was his wife's dowry. It was, however, Bertha, rather than the pottery, which attracted Feuerbach; their courtship was idyllic and their married life was happy and contented. Even the beauteous and much-sought Johanna Kapp, who broke a number of famous hearts—including that of the novelist Gottfried Keller—broke not a single Bruckberg plate. Her desperate love for Feuerbach drove her to insanity and death; Feuerbach and his wife lived happily on.

In 1838 Feuerbach published his *Pierre Bayle*, and in 1839 his *Philosophie und Christenthum* ("Philosophy and Christianity"), as well as a work on Hegel. These gained him some repute and following among the critical younger philosophers. Then, in 1841, he published his *Das Wesen des Christenthums* ("The Essence of Christianity"). This was his chief work; with it Feuerbach's star reached its zenith, and for the ensuing decade he bestrode the philosophical world like a Colossus; even his enemies admitted it. Two years later he wrote his *Grundsätzen der Philosophie der Zukunft* ("Bases of the Philosophy of the Future"). His influence spread. He came into contact with Strauss, Ruge, Herwegh, Marx, Engels, and others; he carried on a voluminous correspondence with leaders of thought in all domains. Yet all the while he lived a simple, isolated life, his only concession to the world being a penchant for vari-coloured waistcoats and flamboyant neckties. (The poet Herwegh said he had the air of a Bavarian lieutenant.)

Although Feuerbach played no direct role in affairs

political, his religious rebellion carried over, as we shall see anon, into politics in the doctrines of some of his followers. For this reason he was a minor hero to the revolutionists of 1848. Despite the miserable collapse of their efforts, Feuerbach was able to emerge from his seclusion during the years 1848 and 1849 and was permitted, under the Diet of Frankfort, to give public lectures on religion and the philosophy of the future to a mixed audience of workers and intellectuals in Heidelberg. After a brief emergence Feuerbach returned to Bruckberg and isolation. His star by then had passed its zenith; many of his friends were in exile; others had moved beyond him and were preoccupying themselves with problems in the more general social realm in the light of the then emerging philosophy of Marxism, itself semi-Feuerbachian in origin, but meta-Feuerbachian in structure and conclusions. In 1857 Feuerbach wrote his *Theogonie*, considered by himself and his friends as his most important work, but considered by history to be less important than his *Wesen des Christenthums*. In 1860 the Bruckberg porcelain factory failed and Feuerbach had to remove to Nuremberg. There he lived, his modest living inadequately supplied by the voluntary subscriptions of his friends the world over, publishing in 1866 his last work, *Gott, Freiheit, und Unsterblichkeit* ("God, Freedom, and Immortality").

From that time on Feuerbach's health began to fail him; during his last days he was racked with pain; and on September 13, 1872, death—which he had long regarded as a natural, human, and proper end—came to claim him. So passed a simple and modest man. He had, as we shall see, consecrated his entire life to exposing all the dogmas, illusions, and authorities which seek, in the words of Nietzsche, to divinize or diabolize natural and human things.

*   *   *   *   *

It has been said that Feuerbach belongs to Hegel as much as the beaker of hemlock belongs to Socrates, that "Feuerbach was Hegel's fate."[1] This is thoroughly true, both politico-historically and philosophically. The Hegelian system prepared the way; Hegel had to have a Feuerbach. Whether, without a Hegel, there still would have been a Feuerbach is another question. It is our contention, however, that there would have been, for the social and cultural milieu which produced Kant, Fichte, Hegel, and Schelling also produced the social and cultural contradictions which gave impetus and meaning to the philosophies of Feuerbach, Strauss, Ruge, and Marx.

The neo-Hegelian Croce is un-Hegelian in attempting to divide Hegel. He asserts that there are two Hegels, the historical and the philosophical. He admits, and seems to regret, the Hegel who was a prop and bulwark to conservative Prussian absolutism. And so he says that this Hegel "must not be confused with the philosopher Hegel who alone belongs to the history of Philosophy."[2] This type of Hegelianism, in general, looks down its nose at those—i.e. the Young Hegelians—who, we submit, took what was living, threw out what was dead, in the philosophy

<hr/>

[1] Glöckner, *Die Voraussetzungen der Hegelschen Philosophie*, Stuttgart, p. xviii; quoted by Hook, op. cit., p. 220.

[2] Croce, *What is Living and What is Dead of the Philosophy of Hegel*, London, 1915, p. 66.

of Hegel. But it was exactly the fact that Hegel, like peace, is indivisible which made inevitable Young, or left, Hegelianism. To be sure, Hegelianism is subject to interpretations which lead to diametrically opposite positions. Hegel's Logos led to directly theistic interpretations, on the right; his historical dialectic led to interpretations regarded as directly atheistic. But in neither direction can we make out a major dualism in the Hegelian system. The whole trend of Hegelianism leads to an identification, not a division, of philosophy and history.*

It is in no sense our purpose here to go into an exhaustive discussion of Hegel, to whom we shall have occasion to refer several times throughout the course of this writing. It is necessary, nevertheless, to devote a few sentences to him by way of preliminary.

Hegel cannot be condensed into a book, much less a sentence. An English Hegelian has, however, packed a good deal into the following few words: "As Aristotle—with considerable assistance from Plato—made explicit the abstract universal, that was implicit in Socrates, so Hegel—with less considerable assistance from Fichte and Schelling—made explicit the concrete universal, that was implicit in Kant."[1] The concrete universal and the dialectic of opposites were Hegel's contribution to philosophy, which latter he defined as the "thinking view of things."[2] He sought to transcend all the dualisms that have plagued the history of philosophy—between mind and matter, form and content, conscience and law, individual and society—by pre-

* cf. Hegel's *Philosophy of the State and of History.*
[1] Stirling, *The Secret of Hegel,* London, 1865, p. 11.
[2] "*denkende Betrachtung der Gegenstände,*" from his *Encyclopaedia.*

senting them all as equally objective aspects of a continuing process. The origin and point of repair of all things is the Absolute Idea, derived from the first, simple, initial concept of Being. By means of the dialectic, the Absolute—mind, form, conscience, self—is self-alienated into matter, content, law, society. The system is pan-logistic. The dialectic pervades all thought and existence. It is characterized by the triadic law of the thesis, preliminary affirmation and unification; the antithesis, negation and differentiation; and the synthesis, final and higher unification. The subject matter, systematically speaking, of the thesis is logic and the phenomenology of spirit, of the antithesis, nature, law, and history; and of the synthesis, art, religion, and philosophy. The creation in this system is immanent. The *deus* is *in*, not *ex*, *machina*. Theoretically, the only *a priori* in the system is the initial Being, from which Hegel pretends to induce the Absolute Idea. There is no transcendence in the system, no externally derived postulates of the reason. There are no limitations, as with Kant, to the activity of the mind.* "The real is the rational; the rational, real," according to the famous Hegelian dictum. Nothing is inscrutable; the Absolute is self-revealing. From the indiscriminate empirical facts of the world we can immediately draw appropriate metaphysical axioms. Man, the self-alienation of the Idea, is significant only in so far as he *is* the self-alienation of the Idea; he becomes swallowed up in the Higher Synthesis. Religion is the presentation of this system in a sentimental form; God is the system. And philosophy is the more explicit, intellectual appraisal of the

---

* But there is not, as there was with Kant, a more universal way, than the individual, of knowing.

whole, by implication one step higher than religion; thus Hegel—whom his critics accuse of sucking the world from his finger tips by a process of logical deduction—can be construed as occupying a place in the cosmic and universal scheme one step higher than God.*

The preceding paragraph, save, perhaps, for the last sentence, states the position more or less as might many an Hegelian. From it three things stand out: The sweeping direct relation between the progress of the Idea and that of the world, by means of the dialectic; the deification of practically everything that exists, from Hegel's pencil (a self-alienation of the Idea) to the Prussian state under Frederick William III—by the "All that is real is rational" formula; and the lowly, subordinate, insufficient role played by man. History makes man, rather than man making history, with Hegel; there is no "monadology"† in the system.

It was quite natural that the continuators of Hegel should travel in two directions. Those to whom the theological aspect, the literal translation, of Hegelianism appeared paramount; to whom the practical political, as well as theoretical, absolutism of the system was agreeable; who conceived the Logos of the system as all-important—those made up the Hegelian right.‡ On the other hand, there were those to whom the idea of progress, the ideological processus, of the system was paramount. These tended to deny

* For an analysis of this relation between Hegel and God, see Janet, in Janet and Seailles, *Histoire de la Philosophie*, Paris.

† The Leibnitzian expression is borrowed, in this connection, from M. Charles Werner.

‡ Kuno Fischer, Stirling, and Bosanquet might be named as some of the leading spirits in this group.

the theological value of logical forms, the development of which they ascribed to the human thinker rather than the self-revealing Absolute. This led to the conception that the Absolute was man-made, and, since a mere logical series cannot be construed as the author of nature, the consequent starting-point was the material universe. Those who developed Hegelianism in this sense were the Hegelian left, or Young Hegelians. The system with them ceased to be an idealization of religion, and became instead a natural theory, prominently operated and explained by the Hegelian logic.

The foregoing sketches, in a most summary way—purposely stressing differences rather than similarities—the background upon and against which the pre-eminent left continuator of Hegel, Feuerbach, built his philosophy. In 1839 he wrote his *Zur Kritik der Hegelschen Philosophie* ("Towards a Critique of the Hegelian Philosophy"). Although this belongs to the middle period of Feuerbach's work, we may be permitted briefly to comment upon it in order to fill out a part of the just-sketched cartoon.

At the outset, Feuerbach places the situation in focus by using Hegel against Hegel. It had been the contention of the latter that, since truth is seen only through the working out of the dialectic, no philosophy had the right to lay claim to absolute truth. Each philosophy appears at a given time, with a given presupposition or set of presuppositions; each meets specific problems set by tradition or its cultural milieu. Correct. The Hegelian philosophy also arose in a determinate time, heir to the Kantian philosophical tradition. Therefore, the Hegelian system can no more lay claim to absolute truth than any other historical set of answers. The presuppositions of Hegelianism must, at the command of Hegelianism itself, be examined in the light of others and of its time.

Hegel's system does, in fact, start out with an uncriticized presupposition, the idea of being. Why not, says Feuerbach, start out with particular being, with concrete reality? In Hegel's logic, being had been defined as immediate, indetermined, and identical to itself. But does not this definition presuppose prior definition of the three defining terms? But not only does Hegel not define them; he outlines the whole dialectic upon the assumption that we have agreed with his postulated idea of being. This idea is an abstraction; reality is only in concrete being. He must first of all prove for us the existence of this universal. If he cannot settle for himself the old quarrel between the nominalists and realists, his system is suspect from the beginning.* For common sense, at the outset, replies that there is no other being but defined and limited being. Not only this, for, although Hegel says he starts out with Being, he does in fact start out with that which he seeks to prove, the Absolute Idea. "The beginning with Being is only a formal thing, for it is not the true beginning, the true first thing; the beginning might just as well have been made with the Absolute Idea, for to Hegel even before he wrote his *Logic*—that is, put his ideas in scientific form—the Absolute Idea was a certainty, a direct truth."[1] In short, Hegel pretends to examine the world and, after exhaustively

---

* This is the same difficulty, but stated in different terms, which beset Fichte in his distinction between the pure, absolute Self and the empirical, real self.

[1] Feuerbach, *Sämmtliche Werke*, 1st ed.; vol. ii, p. 209.

searching about, he finds that all may be subsumed under the dialectically operating Absolute Idea. But what he really does is first to define the Idea in all its major particulars, and then spin the whole world out of it. The Absolute Idea is, therefore, a special type of philosophical question-begging epithet.*

Feuerbach's second major criticism of Hegel concerns sense-perception. It is this specific form of being which Hegel neglects. The first chapter of his *Phenomenology* treats sensible certitude. According to Hegel, our senses say "Here is a tree." We take another step and they say "Here is a house." They say: "Now it is day-time"; we wait a minute, and they say "Now it is night." Nothing remains constant under the successive eclipses of these terms "here" and "now." To Hegel these terms represent universals and not particulars; we cannot even express the particular of which our senses give us the illusion. But, replies Feuerbach, language proves nothing. This man is named John; that man is named Peter. But there are also many other men who have these same names. Does it thereby follow that only Johnness or Peterhood have real existence? On the contrary, the reality of a particular is a truth sealed with our blood; it is only language which is the empty sign without reality. Hegel's refutation of reality is only verbal. He says: "You think you see a tree; turn around; the illusion will have disappeared." This is easy

* We must here be allowed to differ from Engels' famous phrase (*Feuerbach*, English ed., p. 23) that Hegel's Idea "is only absolute in so far as he has absolutely nothing to say about it." He has, in fact, absolutely too much to say about it. What he absolutely does not tell us, though, is how he got to his Absolute. For if he had, it might have given his system away.

in the *Phenomenology*, where it is only a matter of writing down some words, but actually it is different. Answers Feuerbach: ". . . in the reality in which I must turn my clumsy body around, the here—even behind my back—proves to be a very real existence. The tree *limits* my back; it *forces* me from the place which it occupies. Hegel has not refuted the here which presents itself as an object of sense-perception distinct from an object of pure thought, but only the logical here, the logical now."[1]

Feuerbach makes short shrift of the philosopher's penchant for fleeing from sense perception. In his preface to the second edition of *The Essence of Christianity* he writes: "I differ *toto coelo* from those philosophers who pluck out their eyes that they may see better; for *my* thought I require the senses, especially sight."[2] This does not mean, of course, that systematic knowledge can be based uniquely on sense-perception. What he is opposed to is the unmediated hiatus which often exists between sense-perception and thought in idealist philosophy. He points out that it is this fact which has tended to make the data of human experience but a phase of Reason, as with Hegel; which has been responsible for dualist epistemology and the manifold problems which have bobbed up in its wake; or which has caused various philosophers to dismiss the external world as illusory and to postulate reality as psychic or spiritual.

The philosophy of Hegel, continues Feuerbach, pretends to be critical. But to be critical a philosophy must at the outset—we are not now speaking about the development of the system—distinguish between the subjective and objec-

---

[1] Feuerbach, loc. cit., p. 214.
[2] Evans' English translation, 2nd ed., p. viii.

tive. In other words, a critical philosophy cannot be allowed to be critical only after its plans have been drawn and its cornerstone laid. Such a philosophy is only superficially critical. It is not critical (to use an excellent, and difficult to translate, French expression) *à fond*—at the basis, with regard to first causes. Take the use of the void with Hegel. This is a crucial term; Hegel speaks of it without analysing it and without seeking its origin. But what is it? It cannot be thought of, for to think is to define. To think, is to think about something. According to Hegel the world was created by God *ex nihilo*, from the void. That is, God created the world from a something which on the one hand has no dimension, but on the other hand contains everything. A critical philosophy should start by being critical here. In fact, adds Feuerbach, Hegel compares the void to the oriental *Tenebra*; he should have seen there the common origin of the conceptions. The Hegelian void, as the antithesis of Being, is the product of the oriental imagination which opposed to life the notion of death as an independent destructive force, and which saw in night, not the absence of light, but an enemy power of day. This conception—as it should, according to the Hegelian philosophy of history —is out-moded and has vanished; it no longer possesses necessary reality. That is, we thought it had vanished, but it appears to have anomalously smuggled itself into Hegel's intellectual baggage, disguised as the void.

The foregoing is a sample of Feuerbach's attack on the critico-speculative* philosophy. We may sum up his attitude to it—indeed, in a large measure, sum up his

---

* "... my work ... is the direct opposite of speculation, nay, puts an end to it by explaining it."—Ibid., p. ix.

whole initial outlook—in the following somewhat verbose quotation:

"I do not generate the object from the thought, but the thought from the object; and I hold *that* alone to be an object which has an existence beyond one's brain. I am an idealist only in the region of *practical* philosophy, that is, I do not regard the limits of the past and present as the limits of humanity, of the future; on the contrary, I firmly believe that many things—yes, many things—which with the short-sighted pusillanimous practical men of to-day, pass for flights of the imagination, for ideas never to be realized, for mere chimeras, will to-morrow, i.e. in the next century—centuries in individual life are days in the life of humanity—exist in full reality. Briefly, the 'Idea' is to me only faith in the historical future, in the triumph of truth and virtue; it has for me only a political and moral significance; for in the sphere of strictly theoretical philosophy, I attach myself, in direct opposition to the Hegelian philosophy, only to *realism*, to materialism in the sense above indicated."[1]

The preceding indicates, in a general way, the essence of Feuerbach's criticism of, and departure from, Hegelianism. His description of Hegel's role in the history of philosophy remains to be added. The development of absolute idealism is traced by Feuerbach from its neo-Platonic origins down to Hegel, its rapports with Christianity being demonstrated and emphasized. Hegel is characterized as the last, but not least effective, of the major Christian apologists. The Hegelian philosophy, Feuerbach concludes, "is the last refuge, the last rational support of theology. Just as once

[1] Ibid., p. viii.

upon a time the Catholic theologians were *de facto* Aristotelians in order to combat Protestantism, to-day the Protestant theologians are *de jure* Hegelians in order to combat 'atheism.' "[1]

In this whole criticism it may be seen that Feuerbach, like his French contemporary Auguste Comte, is in revolt against the co-existence of, and lack of rapport between, theological thought and scientific thought. These two philosophers, although in no sense active collaborators, did, in their own time, play analogous roles in their respective countries. Their essential similarity may be easily noted by juxtaposing Comte's law of the three states—the theological, the metaphysical, and the positive—to Feuerbach's frequently quoted aphorism: "God was my first thought; Reason my second; Man my third and last thought."[2] Both of them sought to re-establish the coherence which had been lost by the separation of the scientific or human on the one hand and the theological, transcendental on the other. There are, however, certain differences between the two points of view which must be noted. Comte was a sociologist. He sought to restore a body of doctrine in order to re-establish the social and spiritual harmony which he believed to have existed in the Middle Ages. The anarchic condition of economic society* drove him to consider, almost exclusively, the need for a new social unity. Feuerbach, on the other hand, thought less about the external unity of man than his internal unity, and was inclined to

---

[1] Feuerbach, *Sämmtliche Werke*, 1st ed., vol. ii, p. 262.

[2] Ibid., p. 410.

* Biographers of Comte have remarked upon the fact that, when only nineteen years of age, he could not enjoy himself at a *soirée* in Paris for thought of the thousands of hungry citizens in the capital.

consider individual faith (not in a theological sense, however) rather than social works. Comte's personal background was Catholic; Feuerbach's Protestant. Each had, to a certain extent, the characteristic way of looking at things of his religious background.

Both Comte and Feuerbach were positivists,* in the sense of being opposed to speculative and transcendental metaphysics. Comte, however, sought to universalize the rigorous method of science by the study of society; while Feuerbach sought the same unity via the reform of religion. Comte was a scientist and mathematician who, proceding from the Cartesian tradition, insisted upon a new classification of the sciences; he ended up, analytically speaking, at the field which he was to define and to which he was to consecrate his life, i.e. sociology. Feuerbach, on the other hand, although he had studied science and in his works demonstrated considerable knowledge thereof, began and ended by seeking for humanity a new, purified religion. Another point of difference: Feuerbach began with institutional religion, and, throughout his life, worked more and more away from institutionalism, founding no sect or church, nor wishing to. Comte, on the other hand, tended to institutionalize his insights toward the end of his life, progressing, from this point of view, in the reverse direction from Feuerbach. Thus, although the same metaphysical dilemma provoked both men to attempt the same resolution, they lived and worked in virtually different worlds.

* This term cannot, however, in German philosophical parlance, be applied to Feuerbach. (The German positivists were partisans of the positive religions or disciples of the positive philosophy of Schelling.) Feuerbach is, nevertheless, generally referred to as a positivist by historians of philosophy.

Before proceeding farther, it must be underlined that, from Feuerbach's point of view, religion and philosophy are identical. Feuerbach has often been held to be exclusively a religious psychologist and consequently has been glossed over by philosophers; and, conversely, he has sometimes been held to be a philosopher who merely happened to be an atheist and has therefore been avoided by religionists and theologians. Just as Hegel insisted that religion and philosophy were identical in content and differ only in form, so Feuerbach contended that the content of religion and philosophy are the same and that they differ solely in that the objects of the former are sensuous and imaginative while those of the latter are conceptual and abstract. To Hegel, however, the content is intellectual; to Feuerbach it is essentially emotional. Therefore, while it is true that Feuerbach insisted that his writings are only concerned with "religion and theology and whatever is connected with them,"[1] the significance of these spreads over a far greater area than is habitually connoted by the term religion. It is, in fact, as wide as humanity proper. For it was essentially in humanity that Feuerbach was interested. "Erudition and philosophy," he said, "are to me only the means by which I bring to light the treasure hid in man."[2]

With the foregoing in mind, we shall avoid further comment of a general nature and proceed immediately to the heart of our subject. This we do deliberately. Consideration of Feuerbach is far too often limited to the enunciation of one or two of his more euphonious aphor-

---

[1] Feuerbach, *Sämmtliche Werke*, 1st ed., vol. viii, p. 6.
[2] Feuerbach, *The Essence of Christianity*, p. xvi.

isms, coupled with an indictment either from the point of view of religious orthodoxy or with one or two of Engels' brilliantly biting sentences torn from context. The result is calculated to provoke either a tolerant smile or a less tolerant guffaw. In consequence we shall, in respect both to ourselves and to Feuerbach, commence with a direct consideration of his most important work, reserving for further consideration his place in the history of philosophy and the striking of a balance in the light of the best of present-day insights on the problems with which he dealt.

Chapter II

THE ESSENCE OF CHRISTIANITY

I

"It is not a question of inventing, but of discovering; it is not a question of proving or refuting, but of explaining. It suffices, therefore, to translate correctly, faithfully, the text of the Christian religion, to explain in good German and in an intelligible fashion what is said in the coloured language of the oriental imagination. That, simply, is what the author of *The Essence of Christianity* wished to do."[1]

Thus does a competent French commentator sum up the task which Feuerbach set for himself in his major work, originally to be entitled, according to Grün, *Know Thyself.* The method is simple: analysis of original Christianity, unadulterated by the institutional trappings which commenced to vitiate the simple teachings of Christ from the time of Constantine onwards. "He lets the believers speak themselves. But he admits only the testimony of true Christians. Christianity had its classic period; it is to this period that we must go back. We must take but an abstract of the cowardly, characterless, comfortable, literary, flirtatious, Epicurean Christianity of the modern world, and reflect upon the time when the bride of Christ was yet a

[1] Lévy *La Philosophie de Feuerbach*, Paris, 1904, p. 93.

chaste and unspoiled virgin, before she had woven into her heavenly bridegroom's crown of thorns the roses and myrtle of pagan Venus—way back when she was poor in earthly treasure, but too rich and happy to enjoy her other-worldly love in secret."[1]

Or read it in the words of Feuerbach himself, who says that his analysis "has no pretension to be anything more than a close translation, or, to speak literally, an empirical or historico-philosophical analysis, a solution of the enigma of the Christian religion. The general propositions which I premise in the Introduction are no *a priori*, excogitated propositions, no products of speculation; they have arisen out of the analysis of religion; they are only, as indeed are all the fundamental ideas of the work, generalizations from the known manifestations of human nature, and in particular of the religious consciousness—facts converted into thoughts, i.e. expressed in general terms, and thus made the property of the understanding."[2]

The conclusions at which Feuerbach arrives in this his *magnum opus* can be stated briefly. Taking as point of departure his criticism of Hegel which reverses the relation established by the latter between the Idea and reality, Feuerbach investigates the Christian religion. He shows that religion is the product of man, who creates God in his own image, incarnates in Deity his own nature, needs, and hopes. Man assigns as attributes to God the outstanding qualities of the human species. The fault of religion, therefore, has been to despoil man of his own nature in exteriorizing in God

---

[1] Lévy, *La Philosophie de Feuerbach*, Paris, 1904, pp. 93–4.

[2] Feuerbach, *The Essence of Christianity*, translated from the 2nd German ed. by Marian Evans; 2nd ed., London, 1881, p. vii.

what really belongs to, is the essence of, humanity. The existence of God being illusory, man, unaware of what has happened, becomes a thoroughly egoistic being, divorced from the essential indwelling communal spirit of his species. In order to give back to man his true collective being, the religious illusion must be dissipated; that which man has unwittingly taken from himself and assigned to God must be reintegrated into present reality. Theology must be reduced to anthropology; love of humanity must be substituted for love of God.

The introduction to *The Essence of Christianity* is the statement of this thesis; the rest of the book is its elaboration and proof. The rest of this chapter shall be devoted to a more detailed statement and analysis of this thesis, using, in general, Feuerbach's idiom. But first a word about Feuerbach's presentation.

Feuerbach differs from the classical German philosophers both in his method of approach and in his method of exposition. His is no system *à la* Kant or Hegel. His is rather a chain of loosely-linked aphorisms, all tending to demonstrate his main point, but doing it often in a very unsystematic fashion. Feuerbach is the mad painter rather than the skilled draughtsman. Hence he is often inspirationally extraordinary but, in the technical philosophical sense, almost ridiculous. The two decades of highly abstruse Hegelianizing in which German philosophers preceding Feuerbach had immersed themselves provided the excuse, if not the justification, for Feuerbach's style. In the not quite charitable but very cogent words of Lange, "To a clear logic Feuerbach never attained. The nerve of his philosophizing remained, as everywhere in the idealistic epoch, divination. A 'consequently' in Feuerbach does not, as with Kant and Herbart, carry the force of a real, or at least intended, inference of the understanding, but it means, as with Schelling and Hegel, a leap to be taken in thought; and therefore his system, too, floats in a mystic gloom which is by no means adequately illuminated by the emphasis put upon sensibility and picturableness."[1]

If the preceding expresses Feuerbach's style, from the point of view of a great and serious student of philosophy, rather invidiously; it is only giving him his due also to quote from another no less renowned, but differently qualified, individual. In a letter to Feuerbach dated February 12, 1865, Edward Vaillant quotes Proudhon—who had just read Roy's translation of *The Essence of Christianity* —as having said to him, "That is a book which a philosopher ought to be proud of having written; it is a long time since I have read anything so truly fortifying. . . . Before, I saw in him a great thinker; now I see in him a great philosopher; and, what is more, a writer, for he knows how to laugh and joke excellently—which I find but rarely among the Germans."[2]

*　　*　　*　　*　　*

In considering the essential nature of man, Feuerbach finds the basis of religion to exist in the difference between man and the brute.* The difference, according to Feuerbach,

---

[1] Lange, op. cit., vol. ii, p. 247.

[2] cf. Grün, *Ludwig Feuerbach in seinem Briefwechsel und Nachlass*, Leipzig, 1874, vol. ii.

* Only in ignorance of the state of the natural history of a century ago do people smile at Feuerbach's considering for a moment whether "to the elephant, among other laudable qualities, the virtue of religiousness" should be attributed. He found, happily, that the scientist Cuvier assigned,

is to be found in consciousness, of which he says: "Consciousness in the strictest sense is present only in a being to whom his species, his essential nature, is an object of thought."[1] Religion is identical with this distinctive character of man, is identical with man's consciousness of his own nature. Religion, however, is consciousness of the infinite (here accepted in its vulgar, rather than logical, definition by Feuerbach). But this, too, is boiled down to human terms. "The consciousness of the infinite is nothing else than the consciousness of the infinity of the consciousness; or, in the consciousness of the infinite, the conscious subject has for his object the infinity of his own nature."[2] The infinity of the human consciousness must be accepted, for a finite consciousness is only instinct, which appertains, by previous definition, uniquely to animals.

What further or more specific difference do we note between men and the brutes? They may be subsumed under the triad of reason, will, and affection.[3] But these, asserts Feuerbach, are not powers which we possess, for without them we would not be what we are. They are the constituent elements of man's nature, which he neither possesses nor creates. It is only through the power of these that man has the power to transcend himself. "When thou sinkest into deep reflection, forgetting thyself and what is around thee, dost thou govern reason, or is it not reason which governs and absorbs thee?"[4]

"on the strength of his personal observations, no higher grade of intelligence to the elephant than to the dog."—*The Essence of Christianity*, p. 1.

[1] Ibid., p. 1.   [2] Ibid., pp. 2–3.

[3] "To will, to love, to think, are the highest powers, are the absolute nature of man as man, and the basis of his existence."—Ibid., p. 3.

[4] Ibid., p. 4.

Here one might pause to consider whether this hiatus between man, and his reason, will, and affection is psychologically necessary. Certainly, in establishing it thus categorically, Feuerbach leaves his system—to the extent to which it may be called a system—open for the intrusion of elements which threaten his independence from Hegelian idealism. Let it suffice for the moment to note here that the drive toward materialism which Feuerbach started was meta-Feuerbachian, for, as shall be seen increasingly clearly, Feuerbach was in several respects quite as far from materialism as was Hegel.

But let what Feuerbach does with this simply improvised metaphysics* be observed. "Man," he continues, "is nothing without an object. . . . But the object to which a subject essentially, necessarily relates, is nothing else but this subject's own, but objective, nature."[1] This relation is illustrated by the analogy of the solar system. The Sun is a common object, but under separate conditions, to each of the planets. For example, the Sun which lights and warms Jupiter or Neptune has no physical—but only, rather, an astronomical—significance for the Earth. Thus the relation to the Earth is a special relation, deriving from the particular role which the Sun plays in the Earth's life, so to speak. The measure of the light which the Sun possesses as the object of the Earth is also the measure of the distance which determines the peculiar nature of the Earth. "Hence each planet has in its Sun the mirror of its own nature."[2]

Just so man becomes acquainted with himself by means

* We use the term "metaphysics" not in its etymological sense but in its simplest philosophical sense, as a theory of existence.

[1] *The Essence of Christianity*, p. 4.   [2] Ibid., p. 5.

of the object which he contemplates; consciousness of the objective is the self-consciousness of man. Thus it is that the physical Universe truly calls to man "Know Thyself." And thus that the first philosophers were astronomers.

"The absolute to man is his own nature. The power of the object over him is therefore the power of his own nature."[1] And likewise the power of the object of feeling is feeling itself; the power of the object of the intellect is the intellect itself; and the power of the object of the will is itself the will. What affects feeling? Only that which conveys feeling, i.e. itself, its own nature. The same goes for will and for thought. Therefore no matter what kind of object we may be conscious of at any given time, we are at the same time conscious of what we have previously defined as our own nature. "We can affirm nothing without affirming ourselves."[2] And since willing, thinking, feeling are the perfections or essences or realities of man's own nature, it is impossible that any of these should perceive themselves as limited powers. "What is finite to the understanding is nothing to the heart."[3]

Experience and Hegel would seem to indicate that, whatever is the definitive aspect of religion, feeling is its essential organ or mode of expression. Feuerbach points out that if feeling is the essential organ of religion, the nature of God can be nothing else than an expression of the nature of feeling. But if feeling is the subjective essence of religion, then the external data of religion lose their objective value. The only value to be found in any religion then is to be found in the direct relation that the symbols, doctrines, and

[1] *The Essence of Christianity*, p. 5.
[2] Ibid., p. 6.
[3] Ibid., p. 6.

practices of that religion bear to feeling. Therefore the monopoly claim of any religion must be denied if it can be shown—as it has been, times without number—that any other object excites the same emotions as are excited by the religion in question. Thus, for example, the claims of a society of political rebels, of a fraternity or lodge, and of Christianity or Mohammedanism must be adjudged in the same light. Because, following our analysis, when feeling is established as the subjective essence of religion, it is the objective essence also.* Thus the professed objective essence of a given religion, although it may be of interest to history or mythology, is of no importance *per se* to the philosophy of religion.

We come to Feuerbach's definition of God. "Thou hast thus no other definition of God than this: God is pure, unlimited free Feeling."[1] (Or even if one must—despite the preceding paragraph—posit an object of feeling, that object is only the essence of pure, non-subjective feeling, and God is the feeling of feeling.)

It is appropriate to interpellate here that Feuerbach has been reviled in a manner *horribile dictu* and with a vocabulary that puts Billingsgate to shame by those who accuse him of dethroning Deity; yet those same revilers have been unable to attack him at a point so crucial as his definition of God. One of those critics, previously referred to, interestingly reveals the bankruptcy of his criticism on just

---

* Feuerbach asserts that this is admitted, in a backhanded fashion, even by the apologists of transcendental religion, for, with them, "the distinction between specifically religious and irreligious, or at least non-religious, feelings is abolished—a necessary consequence of the point of view in which feeling only is regarded as the organ of the divine."—*The Essence of Christianity*, p. 10.   [1] Ibid., pp. 10–11.

this point. For, after attacking the intellectual denigrators of Deity, he says ". . . it should rather be shown that there is a *religious sentiment*, and that therefore there must be a God."[1] What difference, except verbal, is there between "religious sentiment" and Feuerbach's definition as expressed in the preceding paragraph?

Is Feuerbach an atheist? "Feeling," he replies, "is atheistic in the sense of the orthodox belief which attaches religion to an external object; it denies an objective God— it is itself God. In this point of view only the negation of feeling is the negation of God."[2] And he virtually dares the reader to examine his feelings, in his concluding paragraphs on the essential nature of man. "Fettered by outward considerations, still in bondage to vulgar empiricism, incapable of comprehending the spiritual grandeur of feeling, thou art terrified before the religious atheism of thy heart. By this fear thou destroyest the unity of thy feeling with itself, in imagining to thyself an objective being distinct from thy feeling, and thus necessarily sinking back into the old questions and doubts—is there a God or not?—questions and doubts which vanish, nay, are impossible, where feeling is defined as the essence of religion. Feeling is thy own inward power, but at the same time a power distinct from thee, and independent of thee; it is in thee, above thee, it is itself that which constitutes the objective in thee— thy own being which impresses thee as another being; in short, thy God."[3]

[1] Maccall, op. cit., p. 117. Italics mine.
[2] Feuerbach, op. cit., p. 11.
[3] *The Essence of Christianity*, p. 11.

II

In the ordinary perceptions of the senses, one's consciousness of the object of consciousness (i.e. one's awareness of the balloon barrage which he sees, of the perfume which he smells, or the entrecôte which he tastes) is discrete and separable from consciousness of self. The crux of our problem in the analysis of the essence of religion considered generally is this: religious perceptions are not so; in religion the consciousness of object and consciousness of self coincide. The object of the senses is outside us. The object of religion is inside. St. Augustine states it: "God is nearer, more related to us, and therefore more easily known by us, than sensible corporeal things."[1] The existence of various types of pantheism and immanent theism bear witness to this fact. Therefore, "Consciousness of God is self consciousness; knowledge of God is self knowledge. By his God thou knowest the man, and by the man his God; the two are identical."[2]

But ignorance concerning this relation is fundamental to the peculiar nature of religion, which is man's first, indirect form of self-knowledge. It is the childlike condition of humanity; "but the child sees his nature—man—out of himself; in childhood a man is an object to himself, under the form of another man.* Hence the historical progress of religion consists in this: that what by an earlier religion was regarded as objective, is now regarded as subjective; that is, what was formerly contemplated and worshipped as God

[1] Augustine, *De Genesi ad litteram*, I, v.c. 16.
[2] Feuerbach, op. cit., p. 12.
* Who has not heard a child speak of himself in the third person?

48

is now perceived to be something *human*. What was at first religion becomes at a later period idolatry; man is seen to have adored his own nature. Man has given objectivity to himself, but has not recognized the object as his own nature: a later religion takes this forward step; every advance in religion is therefore deeper self-knowledge."[1] But just as ignorance concerning the God- and self-consciousness relation is fundamental to the peculiar nature of religion, so does no religion understand its own historical progress. Each supposes itself immune, on a higher level than those preceding; each imputes only to other religions, but not to itself, what is the character of religion in general.

Upon the basis of the foregoing, Feuerbach seeks to prove that "the antithesis of divine and human is altogether illusory, that it is nothing else than the antithesis between the human nature in general and the human individual; that, consequently, the object and contents of the Christian religion are altogether human."[2] The fact that the divine being is only the objectivation, abstraction, or purification of the human being means that the attributes of the divine nature are therefore attributes of human nature. Leibnitz in effect agreed to this when he wrote "The perfections of God are those of our souls, but He possesses them without limits. In us there is some power, some knowledge, some charity, but these exist completely in God."[3] In general, it might be said, this is admitted with reference to the attributes of Divine Being but not to the substantive itself. The negation of the subject is considered atheism, but the

---

[1] *The Essence of Christianity*, p. 13.
[2] Ibid., pp. 13–14.   [3] Preface, *Theodicy*.

negation of the predicates is considered as being realistic, especially in the present day. But, Feuerbach stresses, that which has no predicates or attributes or qualities has no effect upon the individual; and whatever has no sensible effect upon the individual is for that individual non-existent. In short, to deny all the qualities of a being is tantamount to denying the being itself. The theologist's answer to this, as is well known, is that God is indefinable, inscrutable, unknowable. But to the truly religious man, for whom God is a positive, real being, this answer is not exactly satisfactory.

This theological answer, in fact, gives God a self-contradictory existence. Through it, man excuses himself to the vestiges of his religious conscience for his having forgotten God and having become absorbed in the world, thereby denying God practically but not theoretically. But this theoretical existence "does not affect or incommode him; it is a merely negative existence . . . a state of being which, as to its effects, is not distinguishable from non-being."[1]

Another denial of God stems from the necessity of positing finite characters to divine being so that, should we meet God on the street, so to speak, we would know him. Thus a distinction is made between what God is defined to be in himself and what he is to any subject. Such a distinction is untenable and unfounded, for—here Feuerbach uses an epistemologically idealist argument from the supernaturalists he is combating—"I cannot know whether God is something else in himself or for himself than he is for me; what he is to me is to me all that he is."[2] To illustrate

[1] *The Essence of Christianity*, p. 15.   [2] Ibid., p. 16.

the point: If God were an object to the bird, he would be a winged being, for to the bird the winged condition is doubtless the highest and best of all conditions. It is scarcely thinkable that the bird would say "To me God appears as a bird, but what He is in Himself I do not know." Take from the bird the conception of bird-nature and you rob him of the conception of the highest being. How, then, could he ask whether God in Himself were winged? "To ask whether God is in Himself what He is for me, is to ask whether God is God, is to lift oneself above one's God, to rise up against Him."[1] This point, difficult to refute if one accept the subjective idealist epistemological presupposition involved (which many, if not most, supernaturalists do), is brilliantly illustrated in like wise by a satirical poem of Rupert Brooke's, showing how what might be called "the ichthyocentric predicament" conditions the eschatological conceptions of the fish.

Throughout the history of religion, whenever the idea that the religious predicates are only anthropomorphisms has arisen, so has doubt. Only timorousness has prevented our going the rest of the way and negating the subject. Timorousness and the fact that the subject, the existence of God, does not to us generally appear an anthropomorphism because its conception is involved necessarily in our own existence as subjects. The predicates of deity, however, do appear anthropomorphisms because theirs is but a contingent necessity. That is, the necessity that God should be wise, good, kind, or any other predicate that a given religion may want to give Him, does not seem identical with man's being, but rather evolved by his self-

[1] *The Essence of Christianity*, p. 17.

consciousness, by the activity of his thought. But, following the argument indicated above, the distinction is only apparent. The necessity of the subject lies only in the necessity of its predicates; or—a purely verbal proof— existence is presupposed when it is "predicated." Subject and predicate may, in fact, be distinguished only as existence and essence.

What is proved by this? Only that the certainty of God is in itself no immediate certainty; it depends on the certainty of the qualities of God. To the Christian the certainty of God is that of a Christian God; to a Tibetan Buddhist the certainty of God is that of Padma Sambhava; yes, and to a humanist, the certainty is that of a humanist God. No man can, for example, take umbrage at the nature of his God, because he can conceive of God under no other qualities, to him these qualities are a virtual certainty, a divine reality. "The reality of the predicate is the sole guarantee of existence."[1]

In general, man unreflectively identifies truth and reality. What man thinks is true, he also considers real, because, originally, only the real is true. (The word "true" here is used not in any metaphysical sense, but only in simple opposition to chimeras, fancies, dreams.) Originally man makes truth dependent upon existence. Then he identifies the two; upon pulling them apart again he unconsciously equates them; subsequently, existence depends upon truth. Therefore God exists for us because he is conceived for us under conditions which to us are the truth. He draws his existence from the same reservoir in which we have deposited his attributes. He exists because of them; without

[1] *The Essence of Christianity*, p. 19.

them he is not. "Take away from the Greek the quality of being Greek, and you take away his existence."[1]

Upon this view, religion increasingly appears to be identical with man's nature. That does not mean, however, that man stands above, is superior to, or even is master of, his conception. Man's religion animates, determines, and governs him. Assuming that religion derives exclusively from man's own nature, "the necessity of a proof, of a middle term to unite qualities with existence, the possibility of a doubt, is abolished. Only that which is apart from my own being is capable of being doubted by me. How, then, can I doubt God, who is my being? To doubt of God is to doubt of myself. Only when God is thought of abstractly, when his predicates are the result of philosophic abstraction, arises the distinction or separation between subject and predicate, existence and nature—arises the fiction that the existence or the subject is something else than the predicate, something immediate, indubitable, in distinction from the predicate, which is held to be doubtful. But this is only a fiction. A God who has abstract predicates has also an abstract existence. Existence, being, varies with varying qualities."[2]

The identity of the religious subject and human predicates is, of course, well illustrated by the history of religion. When man lived in a state of nature, his religion expressed itself in his god or gods of nature, personifying natural forces—rain, sun, fertility, and the like. When tribal life was the dominant social form, henotheism prevailed. When man commenced to inhabit houses, his gods moved into temples. And, as Feuerbach justly remarks, "temples

[1] *The Essence of Christianity*, p. 20. [2] Ibid., p. 20.

in honour of religion are in truth but temples in honour of architecture."[1] Farther along in social evolution, as man has emerged to relative culture, the distinction between what is fitting for him and what is not, has carried over to his gods. Examples in point are the gods of the Greeks, who were hearty trenchermen, paragons of strength, and not inept at the art of love. The dominant god of the war-loving ancient Germans was the great and fearful Odin (who properly disappeared into the limbo of discarded gods only to be recalled and refurbished for atavistic Nazism). And similarly, throughout the history of religion, do we find that the attributes of man determine and define his gods. Not the attribute of the divinity, but the divineness of the attribute, is the first true Divine Being.

Why, then, it might be here interjected, do we not understand how we have created our gods? Why do most men believe that a quality is divine because God has it, rather than that God has it because it is, in a natural sense, divine? Feuerbach answers: "Not until several, and those contradictory, attributes are united in one being, and this being is conceived as personal—the personality thus being brought into especial prominence—not until then is the origin of religion lost sight of; it is forgotten that what the activity of the reflective power has converted into a predicate distinguishable or separable from the subject, was originally the true subject."[2] Secondly, the identity of human and divine predicates has been obscured by a sort of theological trick, which takes advantage of the fact that so great a number of attributes pervade humanity that God has been asserted to possess an infinitude of predicates. Each of us

[1] *The Essence of Christianity*, p. 20.   [2] Ibid., p. 22.

knows only a few of these attributes, i.e. those which are analogous to our own; we know the rest of God's attributes, therefore, only when we are "tuned in"—if that expression may be used—on infinity's wave-length; that is, theoretically, after death. But the mystery of the inexhaustibility of the divine predicates turns out to derive solely from the fact that human nature, because each human being born adds attributes to the human store, can be considered infinite, in a phenomenal (Kantian) sense. Thus the notion of the infinity of God's predicates is a phantasy derived from the sensible world, as well as a conception completely antithetical "with the Divine Being considered as a spiritual, i.e. an abstract, simple, single being."[1]

Thus far we have shown that the subject lies entirely in the attributes of the subject; that the predicate is the true subject. We have also shown that the divine predicates are attributes of human nature. Therefore the subject of those predicates, Divine Being, is also of human nature. *Quod erat*, in a general sense, *demonstrandum*. It is now clear that in religion, man—in his relation to God—"is in relation to his own nature; for to the religious sentiment these predicates are not mere conceptions, mere images, which man forms of God, to be distinguished from that which God is in Himself, but truths, facts, realities. Religion knows nothing of anthropomorphisms; to it they are not anthropomorphisms. It is the very essence of religion, that to it these definitions express the nature of God."[2]

Vulgar anthropomorphism has often insisted that there is a 1 to 1 correspondence between the attributes of God and the attributes of man, between what God has and what man

[1] *The Essence of Christianity*, p. 23.   [2] Ibid., p. 25.

has. Feuerbach denies this relation, insisting that since what is positive in the conception of the divine being can only be human, the conception of man as the object of consciousness can only be negative. "To enrich God, man must become poor; that God may be all, man must be nothing."[1] But man does not himself wish to be anything if, in taking from himself, he can preserve that which he takes from himself in God. This is no species of Spartan self-denial, for what he takes from himself and deposits with God he positively enjoys, and in greater measure. This Feuerbach illustrates in the following justly famed passage:

"The monks made a vow of chastity to God; they mortified the sexual passion in themselves, but therefore they had in heaven, in the Virgin Mary, the image of woman—an image of love. They could the more easily dispense with real woman in proportion as an ideal woman was an object of love to them. The greater the importance they attached to the denial of sensuality, the greater the importance of the heavenly virgin for them: She was to them in the place of Christ, in the stead of God. The more the sensual tendencies are renounced, the more sensual is the God to whom they are sacrificed. For whatever is made an offering to God has an especial value attached to it; in it God is supposed to have especial pleasure. That which is the highest in the estimation of man is naturally highest in the estimation of his God; what pleases man pleases God also . . . The nun weds herself to God; she has a heavenly bridegroom, the monk a heavenly bride. But the heavenly virgin is only a sensible presentation of a general truth, having relation to the essence of religion. Man denies to himself only what he

[1] *The Essence of Christinaity,* p. 26.

attributes to God. . . . Whatever religion consciously denies—always supposing that what is denied by it is something essential, true, and consequently incapable of being ultimately denied—it unconsciously restores in God."[1]

It is for this reason that the thoughts of God are earthly, human thoughts. In exchange for man's having given up to God his personality, God is a person. In exchange for man's ego, God represents a concentration of egoism. This is what Feuerbach meant when he expressed elsewhere, "God can only love himself, can only think of himself, can only work for himself. In creating man, God seeks his own ends, his own glory."[2]

And thus it is that religion denies goodness as a quality of human nature, considering God as the only good—the Good Being. For the nature of man demands as an object a personified goodness. But it is just this fact which gives the lie to the theological doctrine of original sin; the definition of God as good, is itself a declaration that goodness is an essential quality of man. Could one appreciate the Mona Lisa if he had no aesthetic sense? Hardly. Similarly man can appreciate God's goodness only because there is goodness, a moral sense, in him. That which is absolutely opposed to his nature is neither perceptible or conceivable by man. "I can perceive sin as sin, only when I perceive it to be a contradiction of myself with myself—that is, of my personality with my fundamental nature. As a contradiction of the absolute, considered as another being, the feeling of sin is inexplicable, unmeaning."[3]

---

[1] *The Essence of Christianity*, p. 26.
[2] Feuerbach, *Pierre Bayle, Ein Beitrag zur Geschichte der Philosophie und Menschheit*, 1838, p. 107.   [3] *The Essence of Christianity*, p. 28.

The same is true of the allied doctrine that man can of himself do nothing good. If this were true, it would mean that his God must also be without will or action. But only nihilists thus define God. The very declaration of supernaturalist theologists that God acts in a manner explicable to humanity on the basis of his own moral goodness, is an implicit declaration that human activity—than which in life we know nothing higher—is itself divine.

The preceding, then, is an outline of the method by which man unconsciously projects his being into objectivity. This is the involuntary action which is at the core of all religion. Having, then, thus projected himself into objectivity and converted this self-projection into a subject (God), man becomes an object to this subject. And it is from this point that theology steps in and begins explaining things, unaware of—or unwilling to be aware of—what has preceded. Man has, then, in and through God, only himself in view all the time. "It is true that man places the aim of his action in God, but God has no other aim of action than the moral and eternal salvation of man: thus man has in fact no other aim than himself. The divine activity is not distinct from the human."[1] But the divine object plays a very special role in the human activity. For inasmuch as man has come to regard his own activity as objective, inasmuch as he has made the divine subject the repository for certain values, he necessarily receives impulsions and motivations not from himself but from this subject. In contemplating his nature as external to himself, and this nature as goodness, it is, in fact, obvious that the impulse to good can come only from whence he places the good.

[1] *The Essence of Christianity*, p. 30.

God is but man's highest subjectivity, abstracted from himself.

"As the action of the arteries drives the blood into the extremities, and the action of the veins brings it back again, as life in general consists in a perpetual systole and diastole; so is it in religion. In the religious systole man propels his own nature from himself, he throws himself outward; in the religious diastole he receives the rejected nature into his heart again. God alone is the being who acts of himself— this is the force of repulsion in religion; God is the being who acts in me, with me, through me, upon me, for me, is the principle of my salvation, of my good dispositions and actions, consequently my own good principle and nature— this is the force of attraction in religion."[1]

This is Feuerbach's thesis. We shall now consider some of its proofs.

III

It was in no sense Feuerbach's intent to destroy religion. He sought, rather, to reconstruct it. Indeed he once referred to himself as a second Luther.[2] The comparison is apt in the sense that Feuerbach did not proclaim the end of all religion, but only attacked the old in behalf of a new. It was rather at the destruction of theology that he aimed, in accounting for the nature and function of religious experience by means of what has been well called his "psychogenetic method."[3]

---

[1] *The Essence of Christianity*, p. 31.
[2] cf. Bolin, *Ludwig Feuerbach, Sein Werken und seine Zeitgenossen*, Stuttgart, 1891, p. 58.　　　　　　　[3] cf. Hook, op. cit., p. 247.

Feuerbach was the first to approach religion from this point of view, showing how it has its roots in the desires and wants of men, being a necessary and relatively unconscious gratification of man's emotional life, expressed in imagery directly derived from man's objectivation of himself. We have said *unconscious* gratification. Thereto hangs a point.

It would obviously be as fatuous as it is incorrect to assert that Feuerbach was a great psychologist. But it is important to point out that, with reference to the psychology of religion, he saw far beyond his time. He saw, for example, the continuity which exists between the unconscious and the conscious life; it is only because of this continuity that the human origin of religious beliefs and practices is explicable.* And he saw that religion grows not only out of what man has but also out of what he does not have, that human frustrations are at the very base of religion. "Only he who has no earthly parents needs heavenly ones."[1] Asceticism, to paraphrase, is not made by religion, but religion is made by ascetics. And indeed the whole paragraph quoted in the last section on the sexual mortification of the monks, sounds

* It was the scientific establishment and proof of this continuity which was doubtless the greatest contribution of the late great Professor Freud, all of whose theses, as is well known, rest upon just this connection between man's unconscious and conscious selves, his *id* and his *ego*. A serious study of the rapports between Feuerbachianism and Freudianism would probably show numerous points of contact between Feuerbach's shrewd guesses and Freud's proofs. Whoever makes that study might well start with Feuerbach's statement in the preface to *The Essence of Christianity* that "Religion is the dream of the human mind. But even in dreams we do not find ourselves in emptiness or in heaven, but on earth, in the realm of reality."—Page xiii.

[1] *The Essence of Christianity*, p. 73.

very much as though it might have been written by a contemporary psycho-analyst.

This much having been said, it is important to add that Feuerbach did not think of himself as a psychologist but as a philosopher, and as a profoundly religious man. And, though the essential approach of his work is psycho-genetic, the content of his work is catholic. Feuerbach's analysis of the specific aspects of the Christian religion is interspersed with discussions on sociology, hymns sung to the praise of man, indignant refutations of atheism—he characterized it as negative theology—and endless, tedious sermons on love.

We have stated the proposition at the heart of Feuerbach's work, that religion arises out of man's necessary and unconscious deification of himself; and we have observed at some length how he arrived at that proposition. Let us now observe the elaboration of this thesis and certain of its proofs as they are contained in the detailed analysis which makes up the body of *The Essence of Christianity*. This analysis is divided into two parts, the first treating the true or anthropological essence of religion, the second treating the false or theological essence of religion. We shall, however, treat both parts together in order to see simultaneously the negative and positive aspects of this philosophy of religion.

"Religion is the relation of man to his own nature—therein lies its truth and its power of moral amelioration; but to his nature not recognized as his own, but regarded as another nature, separate, nay, contradistinguished from his own: herein lies its untruth, its limitation, its contradiction to reason and morality; herein lies the noxious source of religious fanaticism, the chief metaphysical principle of human sacrifices, in a word, the *prima materia* of all the atrocities, all the horrible scenes, in the tragedy of religious history."[1] In the origin of religion, as we have seen, there is no qualitative or essential distinction between God and man. It is only when religion advances in years and understanding, when consciousness of the identity which exists between the human and the divine begins to dawn, that theology begins and that religion loses its initial vital force. For man's original and involuntary objectivation of himself —thereby unconsciously creating God as a separate being— at the theological stage becomes a reflective, conscious separation of identity. This dichotomy having set in, man commences to be made for the Sabbath, rather than the Sabbath continuing to be made for man. Hence it is correct to say that philosophically, as well as sociologically, the nearer religion stands to its origin the truer and more genuine it is. The latter fact has often been noticed; the former, less frequently so.

Confirmation of the foregoing is seen in even the most cursory analyses of the history of religion. In ancient Judaism, Jehovah differed from the human being only in the duration of his existence. He was entirely similar to man in his qualities and his inherent nature. He even had a human face and figure. Only in the later Judaism was Jehovah separated from man, were allegories fabricated which gave to the old anthropomorphisms a new and separately existential status. So also in Christianity. In the earlier records the supernatural divinity of Christ is less marked than in the latter. Particularly with Paul, as often has

[1] *The Essence of Christianity*, p. 197.

been observed, is Christ considered to be a rather indefinable being, hovering—like Mohammed's coffin—betwixt heaven and earth. He is considered by Paul to possess about the same family tree as the angels; i.e. He was among the first created, but was, nevertheless, created, begotten as are the lowliest of us. True, He was begotten in an especial manner, but—even if we accept the traditional Bible story—at least one of His parents was human. It was only as the Church became institutionalized, as theology walked in, accompanied by the princes of the world, that to Christ was attributed uncreated existence.

What is the first distinctive characteristic which marks the end of simple religion and the beginning of theology? It is when God and man are separated consciously, when the existence of God is made the object of formal proof. Let us take the ontological proof: God is the highest conceivable being. This highest being would not be the highest being if He did not exist, for we could then conceive a higher being who would be superior to Him in the fact that this latter would exist. But the initial idea directly precludes the superiority of the latter. Therefore God exists.

As we have already noted, religion immediately and involuntarily represents man's inner nature as objective, as an external being. At the outset the ontological proof—important for our analysis because it flows from within (man's conception of the highest being conceivable *by him*)—aims simply to prove that religion is right. The contradiction to the religious spirit in the proof of the existence of God lies only in this, that the existence of God is thought of separately, and "thence arises the appearance that God is a mere conception, a being existing in idea only—an appearance, however, which is immediately dissipated; for the very result of the proof is, that to God belongs an existence distinct from an ideal one, an existence apart from man, apart from thought—a real self-existence."[1]

Only, then, in that it presents as a formal deduction the immediate conclusion of religion, is the proof thus far discordant with the spirit of religion—to which God is not a matter of abstract thought but is a present reality. But the proof further errs in supposing that the idea of the highest being can be sufficiently separated from man to be a matter of reflection. For the direct inference of God is itself contained in the idea of the highest conceivable being. The highest conceivable being is not a thought, is not a conception; it is itself immediate reality. Thus the involuntary, necessary God which man cannot help creating religiously, lies Himself inside the first premise of the ontological proof, the establishment of theology. But the fact that the conclusion lies so completely and necessarily in the premise, makes the drawing of the conclusion fatuous, tautologous, and unreal.

The proofs of the existence of God have for their fundamental aim to make the internal external, to divorce it from man. God's existence once thusly proved, He becomes a Kantian noumenal being, a "thing-in-itself." His existence is external to us. But such an existence is less far away from us, esteems Feuerbach, than might at first be thought. "Such an existence is no other than a sensational existence; i.e. an existence conceived according to the forms of our senses."[2] What does a theological proof mean, in short, when it is asserted that God's separate existence is established? It only

[1] *The Essence of Christianity*, p. 199.   [2] Ibid., pp. 199–200.

means that God's existence, "external to us," is established. "But if the externality is only figurative, the existence also is figurative," says Feuerbach, and adds: "Real, sensational existence is that which is not dependent on my own mental spontaneity or activity, but by which I am involuntarily affected, which is when I am not, when I do not think of it or feel it. The existence of God must therefore be in space—in general, a qualitative, sensational existence. But God is not seen, not heard, not perceived by the senses. He does not exist for me, if I do not exist for him; if I do not believe in a God, there is no God for me. If I am not devoutly disposed, if I do not raise myself above the life of the senses, he has no place in my consciousness. Thus he exists only in so far as he is felt, thought, believed in: the addition 'for me' is unnecessary."[1]

Kant, then, was completely right in his maintenance of the fact that the existence of God cannot be proved from reason, but he was wrong in supposing that in so maintaining he was doing something remarkable (if indeed he did; from all evidence he was a modest man). For, in Feuerbach's view, this revolution of Kant's was self-evident. The theological proof of the existence of God transcends the limits of the reason in the same sense in which seeing or hearing or touching or tasting or smelling transcend the limits of the reason. Existence is, in short, proved by the senses alone, not by the reason.

Furthermore, religion, as it is founded on the independent existence of God as an empirical truth, turns out to be a matter of indifference to the inner disposition of man. Which is a contradiction, inasmuch as God is the highest

[1] *The Essence of Christianity*, p. 200.

aspect of man's nature and is thereby unqualifiedly good. The procedure of theology in making God independent of man has divorced God from his attributes. The result has been that the God who has been theologically "proved" to be existent has been largely bereft of his human attributes. These have then had to be unnaturally superadded. But even this has been relegated to a matter of secondary importance; proof of the existence of God has been considered all important. The test has been one of belief. "If thou only believest in God—believest that God is, thou art already saved."[1] No matter, then, whether this God is a really divine being or a master, whether he is a merciful God or a creature of *Blut und Boden*—"the main point is that thou be not an atheist."[2] A direct corollary, then, of the fact that God, removed from his human origins, has to be proved theologically, is that his existence is all important, his attributes are unimportant. And in the train of this separation between God and his attributes have come all the outrages, all the unholy conceptions, all the infamous, senseless, and horrible ideas that have stigmatized the history of theological religion. Whether the Crusades or the Inquisition or the cult of Dr. Alfred Rosenberg,* its roots are the same. Thus belief in the existence of God is compatible with all sorts of immoral actions, just as what theology calls "atheism" is compatible with highly moral actions. Therefore, in the words of Feuerbach, "the belief that God is the necessary condition of virtue is the belief in the nothingness of virtue in itself."[3]

[1] *The Essence of Christianity*, pp. 201–2.   [2] Ibid., p. 202.
* *Der Mythus des Zwanzigsten Jahrhunderts*, Munich, 1930.
[3] Ibid., p. 202.

No, theologues, the belief in God is the belief in a special existence, separate from the existence of man and Nature, an existence which can be proved only in a special manner! But this is a true and living faith only when special effects, personal appearances of God, and miracles *qua* miracles are believed in. "Where, on the other hand, the belief in God is identified with the belief in the world, where the belief in God is no longer a special faith, where the general being of the world takes possession of the whole man, there also vanishes the belief in special effects and appearances of God. Belief in God is wrecked, is stranded on the belief in the world, in natural effects, as the only true ones. As here the belief in miracles is no longer anything more than the belief in historical, past miracles, so the existence of God is also only an historical, in itself atheistic conception."[1]

No, theologues, God is not your theological creature. He is but man's infinite, perfect, positive, strong, good, intelligent,* necessary self.

Let us turn to the form in which Deity is represented— the Trinity. The roots of this concept are explicable from a humanistic, genetic point of view; the theological consequences, on the other hand, are unmeaning, sometimes bordering on nonsense.

Only a God who suffers can suffice for suffering mankind; only a God who feels and wills and loves can suffice for men who feel and will and love; only a being who comprises in himself the whole man can satisfy the whole man. From this fact is born the Trinity, a direct product of our con-

[1] *The Essence of Christianity*, p. 203.
* "God as the antithesis of man . . . is the objective nature of the understanding."—Ibid., p. 34.

sciousness of ourselves in our totality. Theology takes this product as an image, as a similitude of something beyond the Trinity. Religion must take it as the thing itself.

Religion we have previously defined as the feeling of feeling, the consciousness of consciousness. As such, God the Father is *I*. He is, in general, the faculty of the understanding. But the experience of man shows that solitary life is not complete, that the life of the understanding is not the only life. "Participated life is alone true, self-satisfying, divine life—this simple thought, this truth, natural, immanent in man, is the secret, the supernatural mystery of the Trinity."[1] The solitariness of God, the incompleteness of the life of the understanding, are complemented by God the Son, who represents the *Thou*, the idea of love. God the Father and God the Son together represent man's unconscious objectivation of the totality of his being. The Father is his consciousness, his understanding; the Son is his idea of love, of his fellow man. The third person in the Trinity expresses the love of these two divine persons toward each other. The unity of the Son and the Father is the idea of community; itself symbolized as a special personal being.

It is God the Son who first gives warmth to man. God as the *objective* nature of consciousness, feeling, the understanding, is but a neutral repository for values, a cold object of the intellectual eye. It is God as the Son who first becomes an object of feeling, of rapture, and of affection —for the Son Himself is the special creature of the feeling. He is, in the words of Feuerbach, "nothing else than the glow of love, enthusiasm."[2] Furthermore, God as the Son

[1] *The Essence of Christianity*, p. 67. [2] Ibid., p. 68.

is the primitive incarnation, the primitive self-renunciation of God, the negation of God in God. As the Son He has a finite being; He is created. The infinite Father, on the other hand, has no source; He exists *per se*. But God the Father in begetting the Son renounces His exclusive divinity; He humiliates and lowers Himself, evolving within Himself the principle of finiteness and dependent existence. In the Son, then, God becomes man. Not, to be sure, in the first instance (for in the first instance, as we have already seen, He *is* man) but, rather, in the second instance—in which the inward nature, rather than the outward, original form, is the subject of religious analysis. "And for this reason it is as the Son that God first becomes the object of man, the object of feeling, of the heart."[1]

Just as the organ of feeling is feeling itself, so does the heart comprehend only what springs from the heart. God as the Son is close to the human heart, then, not only because he is the Son of God, but because the true—as distinct from constructed, figurative—Father of the divine Son *is* the human heart. The Son is, in short, the divine heart because he is the objectivation of the human heart into a divine being. The Son was given his psycho-genetic birth in exactly the same way as was the Father, but by a different and less easily definable aspect of the human being. Feuerbach calls it the heart or love. (Its metaphysical status is about as uncertain as its psychological or anthropological status. We shall accept it, however, for the purposes of this analysis and until we can inspect it more closely in different surroundings, in the sense in which nineteenth-century psychology might have accepted it.)

[1] *The Essence of Christianity*, p. 68.

The love of God for man is expressed in and through the Son. How can God be the Father of men, how can He love other beings subordinate to Himself, if He does not know what love is in a personal relation, from His own experience, as it were? The inability of the first religious men to envision such a relation led to the unconscious creation by man of God the Son. The Father and Son in the Trinity are, therefore, father and son not in a completely figurative sense, but in a literal sense. Each is religiously real—in its relation to the other. This has been religion's necessary concept.

Not only this. It was, given the above, quite natural that the family should be completed by the reception of a third, and that a feminine person, into the divine constellation; "for the personality of the Holy Spirit is a too vague and precarious, a too obviously poetic personification of the mutual love of the Father and Son, to serve as the third complementary being."[1] The role of the Virgin Mary differs (she plays, for example, a more important part in Catholicism than in Protestantism) in different religious conceptions. But in all of these She is the maternal principle, both with reference to the Father and to the Son. True, the family relation is purified and, if you will, abstracted. This derives in large measure from the fact that in Christianity—for socio-historic rather than religious reasons—the human reproductive relation was regarded as unholy and sinful.* But, nevertheless, an archetype of

[1] *The Essence of Christianity*, p. 70.

* Pre-Christian religion, of course, makes natural genesis play a considerable role. Which tends to prove—if any proof be necessary—that the unholiness of sex is peculiar to Christianity and not to religion in general.

the family relation it is. "The Virgin Mary fits in perfectly with the relations of the Trinity, since she conceives without man the Son whom the Father begets without woman . . . the Holy Virgin is a necessary, inherently requisite antithesis to the Father in the bosom of the Trinity."[1]

In addition, it is important to observe that what might be called the "feminine principle" exists already in the Son. The Father is masculine, active, strong, and even wrathful. The Son is mild, gentle, conciliating, forgiving. "The Son is thus the feminine feeling of dependence in the Godhead; the Son implicitly urges upon us the need of a real feminine being."[2] Indeed, in certain varieties of Jewish mysticism, God is explicitly considered the masculine principle, the Holy Ghost is the feminine principle; and the Son and the world are esteemed to have arisen out of the intermixture of both.

To Feuerbach the entire underlying idea of love is both created by (systole) and stems from (diastole) the mother-son relation—both in human life and in the Trinity. "The love of the son for the mother is the first love of the masculine being for the feminine. The love of man for woman, the love of the youth for the maiden, receives its religious— its sole truly religious consecration in the love of the son for the mother; the son's love for his mother is the first yearning of man towards woman—his first humbling of himself before her."[3]

So much for the Trinity from the standpoint of its

---

[1] *The Essence of Christianity*, pp. 70–1.   [2] Ibid., p. 71.

[3] Ibid., p. 71. It is interesting to note here the extent to which the psychological verity of this suggestion has been borne out by the psychoanalytic investigation of the Oedipus complex, etc.

religious origin. It is nothing else than the sum of the essential fundamental distinctions which man perceives in the human nature. Only when theology takes hold, seeking (as previously observed in discussing the theological attempt to prove the real, totally independent existence of God) to prove the existential reality of the three persons of the Trinity, do irresoluble contradictions set in. Father, Son, and Holy Spirit are asserted to exist. The existence of the three persons, on the other hand, is done away with by the command of monotheism.

What religion affirms as relations, theology asserts to be independent existences. But how does the Son of God make sense without a Father, and vice versa? How can the Trinity be construed, in fact, but relationally? "To require the reality of the persons is to require the unreality of the unity, and conversely, to require the reality of the unity is to require the unreality of the persons. Thus in the holy mystery of the Trinity—that is to say, so far as it is supposed to represent a truth distinct from human nature—all resolves itself into delusions, phantasms, contradictions, and sophisms."[1]

The Trinity, as a theological conception, has been shown to be riven with contradictions. Similarly, Feuerbach analyses the sacraments, showing that though their origin is natural their theological application is sophistry. The Lord's Supper, for example, is agreed by theology to be nothing without a certain state of mind. Nevertheless theology presents the sacrament as something real and external, distinct from the human being. The result is that the true element is made only a collateral thing, a condi-

[1] *The Essence of Christianity*, p. 235.

tion; the imaginary becomes the principal element. The consequences of this subordination of the human to the supposed divine are both superstition and immorality. Superstition, because a thing has attributed to it an effect which does not lie in its own nature, because it is held up as not being what in truth it is. Immorality, because in sentiment the holiness of the action as such is separated from morality; the partaking of the sacrament, regardless of the partaker's state of mind, becomes a holy act. "Such, at least, is the result in practice, which knows nothing of the sophistical distinctions of theology. In general: whenever religion places itself in contradiction with reason, it places itself also in contradiction with the moral sense. Only with the sense of truth coexists the sense of the right and good. Depravity of understanding is always depravity of heart."[1]

The root of this contradiction, which is, in short, the root of the main contradiction in Christian theology, lies in another contradiction—that which exists between faith and love.* The consequences of this contradiction are of particular import to man because the Christian religion is especially distinguished from other religions in giving especial prominence to the salvation of man. For this reason a discussion of this contradiction, delineation of which lies at the heart of Feuerbach's work and is in many respects the most important elaboration and corroboration of his thesis, is important. The Sacraments are in the first instance, as we have just noted, a sensible presentation of another, simpler contradiction. This Feuerbach sometimes inade-

---

[1] *The Essence of Christianity*, p. 246.

* We do not here speak of contradictions in a metaphysical Hegelian or dialectical Marxian sense, but in a strictly logical sense.

quately calls the contradiction of idealism and materialism. At other times he better calls it the contradiction between subjectivism and objectivism. We have seen the roots of this simpler contradiction in our analysis of the essence of religion considered generally. To what greater contradiction does it lead?

The essence of religion, its latent nature, is the *identity* of the divine being with the human (deriving from the simpler contradiction between subjectivism and objectivism in man's unconscious self-objectivation). But the form of religion, or its apparent, conscious nature is the *distinction* between the divine being and the human. That which reveals the basis, the hidden essence, the identity-aspect of religion is love. That which constitutes its conscious form, its distinction-aspect, is faith. Love identifies man with God and God with man; consequently it identifies man with man. Faith, being the expression of the conscious, theological form of religion, separates God from man and vice versa; consequently it separates man from man. "For God is nothing else than the idea of the species invested with a mystical form—the separation of God from man is therefore the separation of man from man, the unloosening of the social bond. By faith, religion places itself in contradiction with morality, with reason, with the unsophisticated sense of truth in man; by love, it opposes itself again to this contradiction."[1]

We have already noted the way in which theology, having speculated on the objectivity of God and therefrom established His independence, has constructed proofs of God's existence. Theology has also demanded faith in God's

[1] *The Essence of Christianity*, p. 247.

independent existence. The attempt to establish this independent existence has had as concomitant an attempt to divorce God and Man. Therefore faith does, in fact, isolate God; it produces in man an inward disunion which in time becomes an outward disunion also; it makes belief in God a law. Opposed to unnatural faith is natural love, which, in Feuerbach's view, has as its end the resolution of the theological contradiction by suppressing it. As faith isolates God, love is an agent of reunion, making God a common being, the love of whom is one with the love of man. As faith commands that God shall be believed in, love asserts freedom, condemning not even atheism—for love itself is atheistic in denying the separate existence of God. "Love has God in itself; faith has God out of itself; it estranges God from man, it makes him an external object."[1]

The divisive role of faith in human affairs is patent. God is an independent personal being—a "who" rather than a "what," as Feuerbach calls it—only through faith.* Theo-

---

[1] *The Essence of Christianity*, pp. 247–8.

* In answer to the counter-claims of the theology of revelation, Feuerbach devotes a chapter to denying that revelation is anything other than a "disingenuous, sophistical, tortuous mode of thought . . . occupied only with groundless distinctions and subterfuges" (*The Essence of Christianity*, p. 122). He shows it to be contradiction with man's sense of truth and morality (cf. when the Jews received from Jehovah the command to steal) and stresses that the idea of revelation is exclusive, having historically come to certain men and not to man; therefore in current religious practice it is essentially a matter of written revelation. But theologians must then admit that the Bible is as profane as any other book, the divine elements of which have to be sifted out of it, just as they might out of any history book. As for believing the revealed character of whatever elements might be picked out, that again boils itself down to a matter of faith.

logically God is God to everyone, but He is immediately God to Christians and only mediately God to heathen, i.e. He is God to them as soon as they give up being heathen and become Christian. Thus Christians are Christians by virtue of their special knowledge of God; their mark of distinction is God. Faith, then, gives man a peculiar sense of his own dignity and importance. The believer finds himself distinguished above other men, exalted above the natural man. He possesses special privileges. He is an aristocrat; the unbeliever a plebeian. He is a capitalist; the unbeliever is a proletarian. The God of faith is the agent of this distinction. "Because faith represents man's own nature as that of another being, the believer does not contemplate his dignity immediately in himself, but in this supposed distinct person. The consciousness of his own pre-eminence presents itself as a consciousness of this person; he has the sense of his own dignity in this divine personality."[1]

The preceding two sentences are in the words of Feuerbach. We get almost the same sense out of the following words of Luther: "I am proud and exulting on account of my blessedness and the forgiveness of my sins, but through what? Through the glory and pride of another, namely, the Lord Christ."[2]

This sort of divine arrogance, born through faith, is equally explicable—but no more socially excusable—in its strictly human content. We see it in the way in which a servant glories in the dignity of his master, even to the extent of wishing to remain a servant in preference to being a master of servants in his own right, upon such occasions

[1] *The Essence of Christianity*, p. 250. [2] Luther, Thesis ii, p. 344.

as economic circumstance might make this latter a concrete possibility. This illustration is apt, too, because it demonstrates the peculiar quality of this divine superiority complex which is a feeling, not in behalf of the self, but in behalf of another. For in faith this arrogance clothes itself in the idea of another person, God, who is only man's projected self. Thus we have again here the characteristic feature of all religion, which changes the naturally active into the passive. "The heathen elevates himself, the Christian feels himself elevated. The Christian converts into a matter of feeling, of receptivity, what to the heathen is a matter of spontaneity."[1] It is thus that the humility of the believer is in fact but an inverted arrogance.

Faith is furthermore specific and imperative. It necessarily expresses itself in dogma, which gives it a formula for what is already inchoate mental expression. And being thus dogmatic, faith is illiberal and prejudiced. It can be this without any internal feeling of self-contradiction, because it has come to identify individual salvation with the honour of God. It is solicitous in this respect as is the conscientious soldier who salutes his officer, in passing him, even when the latter is not looking. Theology, particularly Protestant theology, is quick to deny the charge of illiberalism, pointing to its own tolerance with reference to Friday dinner, Sunday baseball, and related subjects. But these are not in any fundamental sense objects of faith. All theology, even the most "liberal," is illiberal in relation to objects of faith. He who is not for Christ is against Him; that which is not Christian is anti-Christ! Call out the navy.

[1] *The Essence of Christianity*, p. 250.

Kill the mahdi. Smash the rebels—whether they be Mohammedans or Moors or Spanish republicans.*

And what is Christian? This must be absolutely determined; it cannot be free. If the articles of faith are set down
in books, written by authors, handed down in the form of
"incidental, mutually contradictory, occasional dicta";[1]
then dogmatic definition is clearly an external necessity.
The Church as an institution owes its very existence to just
such external necessities. True, there are the "believing
unbelievers" of modern times who—opposing, in the name
of the higher criticism, dogmatic Biblical definitions—think
they have avoided this impasse. But these have moved out
and beyond faith, for when the determinate tenets of faith
are felt as limitations, faith has already disappeared.

From the theological point of view the Church was perfectly justified in adjudging damnation to heretics—unbelievers and atheists; for this condemnation is involved
in the very nature of faith. But the separation of the believing
sheep from the unbelieving goats which is effected by faith
is less neutral than might at the outset be supposed. For to
believe is synonymous with goodness; not to believe, with
badness.† The quality of the individual's life is a secondary
consideration. Faith, narrow and prejudiced, refers all
unbelief to the moral disposition. It is for this reason that

---

* Marxists have rightly been quick to point out that so-called "religious
wars" are generally smoke-screens for struggles for class-economic ends.
They have, however, sometimes underestimated the tremendous power
which religious illusions have brought to bear on given situations. The
Feuerbachian analysis does, we submit, in a large measure explain why.

[1] *The Essence of Christianity*, p. 251.

† cf. Luther's "The Cardinal Wickedness is Unbelief."—Thesis XIII,
p. 647.

Feuerbach saw what he called "a malignant principle" in faith.

In general it might be said that with reference to faith each religion sees the motes in the eyes of other religions, but never the beam in its own. Christians will analyse objectively the limitations of other faiths, smiling at the thought of the poor, deluded Mohammedans who joyously rush to death on their battlefields, but unconscious of the like limitations of their own faith. Faith embodies itself differently in different religions, but the nature of faith as such is always and everywhere the same. Its fundamental characteristic, in practice, is condemnation and anathema. Some religions have exterminated unbelievers with the sword; Christianity burns them up in hell fire.* The essential is the same.

Furthermore, faith is a limitation of its opposite, love. God loves all men, that is, all Christian men. "Love thine enemies" means love your personal enemies, but not, decidedly, public enemies. He who loves those who deny God does himself, by so doing, deny God. "Faith abolishes the natural ties of humanity; to universal, natural unity, it substitutes a particular unity."[1]

Unfettered love, the contradiction of faith, is, in this view, everything that faith is not. It recognizes virtue even in sin, truth in error. It is free in the sense in which reason is free —subject to occasional aberrations because of its weakness, not *intrinsically* restrictive. It unites what faith divides, expressing the indwelling communal spirit of mankind. It

* And sometimes this fire ignites earthly funeral pyres for unbelievers, as in the heretic persecutions of the Middle Ages.
[1] Feuerbach, op. cit., p. 254.

does this because it is itself human; "the love of Christ was itself a derived love. He loved us not out of himself, by virtue of his own authority, but by virtue of our common human nature."[1] Love expresses the essential similarities of men. As such it is cement in the social structure.

Feuerbach waxes almost incoherent singing his pæans of praise to love. He does not thereby become irredeemably mystic and sentimental, as many of his critics accuse him of being. In so doing he is only trying to show how love is all the socially good and positive things which faith is not. He is talking here about pure love, the essence of love, love unrestricted. He speaks about it in an extravagant fashion only because he is trying to tell us what unfettered love would be like. In Christian experience we have no genuine conception of the latter, for it is always qualified by faith. Love never has, so to speak, an opportunity to stretch its wings and travel. Its wings have been clipped by faith.

Love is the positive, faith the negative, element in the Christian religion. Christianity is itself contradictory because it sanctions both the actions that spring out of love and the actions that spring out of faith without love. "If Christianity had made love only its law, its adherents would be right—the horrors of Christian religious history could not be imputed to it; if it had made faith only its law, the reproaches of its antagonists would be unconditionally, unrestrictedly true. But Christianity has not made love free; it has not raised itself to the height of accepting love as absolute. And it has not given this freedom, nay, cannot give it, because it is a religion—and hence subjects love to

[1] *The Essence of Christianity*, p. 266.

the dominion of faith. Love is only the exoteric, faith the esoteric doctrine of Christianity; love is only the *morality*, faith is the *religion* of the Christian religion."[1]

Do we need further proof? Take the most sublime of the Christian dicta: God is love. The contradiction is to be seen in the very statement of the proposition, Love is the predicate, God the subject. The very logical construction tells us that God must also be something distinct from love. Otherwise—and this is the only way the distinction could be done away with—the proposition would be: Love is God.

Does the foregoing mean, then, that Christianity is the battleground of opposing forces and may be compared to the mythical city in which the police force was equally composed of the forces of darkness and light? Not exactly, for it is Feuerbach's implicit contention that—despite the power of love—faith is like the rotten apple in the barrel of good apples. It negatives whatever it touches by putrifying it. "A love," he says, "which is limited by faith is an untrue love."[2] Not a limited or inadequate love, but an *untrue* love.

What consequences can we draw from the entire analysis? Let us, in Feuerbach's own words, review it and see:

"In the contradiction between faith and love which has just been exhibited, we see the practical, palpable ground of necessity that we should raise ourselves above Christianity, above the peculiar standpoint of all religion. We have shown that the substance and object of religion is altogether human; we have shown that divine wisdom is human wisdom; that the secret of theology is anthropology; that the absolute mind is the so-called finite subjective mind.

[1] *The Essence of Christianity*, p. 263. [2] Ibid., p. 264.

But religion is not conscious that its elements are human; on the contrary, it places itself in opposition to the human, or at least it does not admit that its elements are human. The necessary turning point of history is therefore the open confession that the consciousness of God is nothing else than the consciousness of the species; that man can and should raise himself only above the limits of his individuality, and not above the laws, the positive essential conditions of his species; that there is no other essence which man can think of, dream of, imagine, feel, believe in, wish for, love and adore as the *absolute*, than the essence of human nature itself."[1] And, we may add, this latter includes external nature as well as human nature. For man belongs to external nature and external nature to man. It is only, in this view, by a union of man and external nature, as a naturalistic conception, that the super-naturalistic egoism of the Christian religion may be conquered.

So much for the essence of Christianity. The analysis has been cursory, but has, in greater or less detail, covered all important points save one, the question of immortality. To that we shall now turn.

[1] *The Essence of Christianity*, p. 270.

Chapter III

IMMORTALITY

Awareness of the significant problem of immortality exists for philosophers and vulgar empiricists alike. The "fears that I may cease to be" are common to all men, even—in strictly private moments—to materialists who say that immortality is a religious question, that Marx said religion is the opiate of the people, and that they do not want to be drugged.* Even granted the partial truth of their statement, an affirmative answer to the question of immortality is quite as necessary for them as their negative one—both for hortatory purposes and for purposes of analysis and understanding. Especially at the time of writing, when possible sudden death is quite as close to the European citizen as his gas-mask, is the question of immortality a more insistent question for everyone than ever. For emphasis on personal immortality seems to be considered socially necessary as an answer to the mute query posed by the brutal, and—in the minds of many people—not quite meaningful, snuffing out of thousands of young lives which in no sense have realized more than a fraction of their inherent capacities.

It is for this reason important to analyse and assess the

* Which dogma, as Professor Hook has well pointed out, has often acted like an opiate itself on the minds of Marx's followers.

problem of immortality in the light in which one who, we submit, was one of its best analysts, did so a century ago. Having done this, we will be in a position to relate his argument to certain present-day arguments and see where the weight of acceptable evidence falls.

Frau Hegel, one day, asked her husband his opinion on the immortality of the soul. The master, without saying a word, pointed his finger at the Bible.[1] The answer was probably satisfactory to his wife, but it is not likely that it would have been completely satisfactory to the many pilgrims who found their intellectual Mecca in the Berlin auditorium where Hegel lectured. For not a few of them, it seems, were disappointed in the lack of concreteness which characterized Hegel's answer to the question.

If Hegel was mute, however, his system was not. The mixture of hellenism and pantheism which came to make up his philosophy had, in form, begun to knock the props out from under personal immortality in the preceding philosophy of Spinoza. In substance, Hegel's coronation of Reason virtually finished the job. Reason alone was eternal. Individual human life was but an ephemeral antithesis, to be resolved in the higher synthesis which was the Idea. The new and grand philosophy of history left no room for illusion. To man it was not to be permitted to play more than once his puny role. Implacable necessity would chase him from the scene to make room for new self-alienations of the Idea. The Supreme Judge had made whole regimes and phases of history parade before him, to march on to their dialectical doom. It was scarcely conceivable that mere individuals could have right of appeal against this fiat.

[1] Grün, op. cit., I, p. 26.

It was, probably, largely under this magistral sweep of Hegelianism that Feuerbach from his earliest years considered death permanent, irremediable, and irreparable. At the age of twenty-four the young philosopher sustained his *Dissertatio inauguralis* before the faculty of Erlangen.[1] In this he developed the theory of the unity of the reason, author of the human soul and knowledge. Only this unity of the reason did he esteem imperishable. The substance of this doctrine was, of course, far from new. Aristotle, in his famous *De Anima*, had hypostatized three divisions of the soul: the nutritive, the sensible, and the *nous*, or the pure understanding. To Aristotle the faculty of immortality was granted only to the *nous*, eternally—in the Aristotelian dictum—"in act." This doctrine was taken up again in the Middle Ages by Averroes, who from it drew the conclusion that only humanity, but not individual man, was immortal. It is this doctrine of Averroes which Feuerbach takes up in his first thesis. The individual, he asserts, only has value by virtue of his participation in the Idea or in Reason. In the same way nature only has value as a transient symbol of the Spirit which is immanent in it. Only the too subjectivist philosophers, Feuerbach insists, inconsistently accord to the individual personal immortality and attach disproportionate importance to the simple phenomenon of natural death. If, he adds, we wish to represent the absolute equality of men, we have no need either to wander through cemeteries or to turn our eyes skywards. Death, which levels all, is in us. The activity of the Reason is the true immortality; for it is only by thought that we are of the human species; by thought we commune with universal and infinite Reason.

[1] *The Essence of Christianity*, p. 203.

85

The preceding paragraph is but a sketch of what to Feuerbach was but a sketch of what he wanted to write on immortality. For in it he regrets that time and space do not permit of a more extended treatment of the subject. Two years later, in his *Thoughts on Death and Immortality*, he returns to the subject. In this, as well as in his first thesis, the traces of Hegelianism in Feuerbach are much more marked than they are in his later work. It is for this reason doubly interesting to examine in some detail Feuerbach's work of 1830. For it provides a refutation of personal immortality in what might be called the classical style, based on supernaturalist presuppositions. From the point of view of the argumentative aspect of the problem, it is therefore closer to pro-immortalist eschatology. The debaters are, so to speak, on the same platform. Having observed Feuerbach's general line of reasoning in this work, we can then move on to an appraisal of the problem as treated in his later work, noting differences and resemblances. We shall thereafter compare this with the present position.

In the introduction to his *Thoughts on Death and Immortality*, Feuerbach suggests that the belief in personal immortality is a necessary consequence of Protestantism and of modern individualism. The supreme principle of Protestantism no longer being human communion in the unity of the Church, personal faith becomes the touchstone of religion.* The change in Church organization which was a part of Protestantism also meant, in effect, that each

---

* Feuerbach had not at this time enunciated his general doctrine on religion which we have already examined. It is interesting to note, however, the germinal expression of ideas which later became the fundamental ideological structure of *The Essence of Christianity*.

Protestant became his own priest; the Church existed in each Protestant's soul. In order that such an interior church might perpetuate itself, the individual human soul had to be eternal. In different terms, the religious subject had no object but himself; he was self-enclosed. But each subject, having cognizance of his faults and imperfections, needed exterior complements to fill up his self-recognized lacunae and to cover over his imperfections. But not finding these complements in this world, which is imperfect as is man, he sought to imagine them in perfect condition in another world. Obviously one of these projected other-worldly perfections was immortality, not so much because man at the outset feels mortality to be too restrictive to himself, but because these projected perfections had to last until he could get to the other world for the reunion of his personality. But obviously, if these perfections survived the subject's own death, it became but a short step from survival of a given individual's mortality to the idea of immortality in general, as absolute.*

But the crux of the question lies in that these personality-prolongations have no reality, despite the fact that their origins are so easily explicable.

Just as it is true that infinite being is infinite and eternal, so is it true that "everything which is in its being determined and limited is determined and limited also in its existence,

* Here and henceforth we consider immortality as *personal* immortality. The doctrines of chemical immortality, biological immortality, immortality of good works, immortality of influence, etc., are patently on another plane. The doctrine of personal immortality has reference to the survival by the human personality—which, if one be a psychological monist, also means survival by the earthly body—of death. We will return to this point later in the chapter.

and that consequently a particular person lives only in a determined and limited time. Recognize that you are a limited being, and not being in general; and you must recognize that you are *to-day* and not *for all* time."[1] The essence of the limit of one's being is his difference from others; of this difference he cannot in a real sense make an abstraction, because it is a particularity. No more, for example, than one can take from a particular white horse the difference by which he distinguishes himself from a herd of black horses; for if one could, the horse would not simply be a horse of another colour; he would have ceased to exist. And—this is the crucial point—determination and distinction are based exclusively in this real life and are real and possible only in the conditions of the here-now below.

Let us go back a little. "You are only an individual as long as you are capable of feeling. Sensation alone gives to the individual the certainty of his existence."[2] But time is inseparable from sensation. Feeling exists only in a certain, fleeting *now*; it is not indefinitely dispersed. Just as the rays of the sun, concentrated in a single spot, produce flame and burn a given substance; so the concentration of all one's being in a single spot at a given instant lights the fire of sensation in the being. Why, then, is there no perpetual bliss? Because perpetual bliss would no longer be bliss; "sentiment is only sentiment if it is transient."[3] Only where there are interruptions, periods, epochs is there sensation.

---

[1] Feuerbach, *Gedanken uber Tod und Unsterblichkeit*, Leipzig, 1830. The accompanying citations are taken from the authorized edition of Feuerbach's writings on immortality, edited and translated under the title *La Réligion* by Joseph Roy, Paris and Brussels, 1864. This citation is from p. 175.

[2] *La Réligion*, p. 176.

[3] Ibid., p. 177.

Where time ceases, sensation ceases; and with it, individuality. "If, then, you promise an individual a personal existence, sensation, and—above all—eternal bliss in another life where you can abstract time; you are only obeying fantasy, for which everything is possible, and not obeying reason."[1]

Furthermore, determinate personality is not only inseparable from time, it also exists necessarily in space. Where is the space in which individuals will live in the life after death? It must be similar in kind to present space, therefore contiguous and a part of present space.* But space belongs essentially to this life; it is the property of the living; and, since the immortals must live in a place, and since this place is in space, the life which follows death must be the same as that preceding it. Thus if the immortals exist in space—and from the foregoing it seems that they must, unless we are to so loosely define the future life as to rob it, as life, of any significant sense—then they must also exist in time, for we cannot here see how space and time can meaningfully be separated. Not only this. The immortals must also exist with the same sensible attributes and the same conditions as in this life, for time and space are inseparable from these attributes and these conditions. If, nevertheless, the immortals must live in space and time without having to undergo the conditions of other terrestrials, then we are left only to represent them as mathematical figures, as symbolic representatives. But these latter also are to be found here below.

Since, then, the life after death must be the same in all

---

[1] Ibid., p. 177.

* For present space, physically, is all the space that there is.

essential conditions as this life, it is natural that many eschatologists should have given up, in times not long past, the imaginary heaven of romantic dream and decided to transport the next life to some place as concrete as the stars. Although the advances made by astronomical science in recent years have tended to push heaven into the very remotest space, if not completely to dissociate it from inter-stellar connections, the argument which Feuerbach levels against those who in his day seriously believed the locus of the future life to be on one of the planets or fixed stars is not without interest for us to-day. Let us see where it leads.

"This manner of envisaging the stars," he says, "derives from the principle that innumerable bodies would exist in vain were they not peopled; and that thus the wisdom of the Creator or the foresight of Nature, neither of which can do anything useless, would be shown to be in flagrant violation of the law of contradiction."[1] But he who accepts this view must also accept the view that everything in the material world is completely superfluous and unnecessary. Man is obviously right in regarding life as the end of a body. But he is wrong in believing that a star out in space is completely useless if it does not contain everything that the earth contains. It is no more superfluous than most of the things we run into in our daily life. If one accept this narrow teleology, he is further obliged to demand why God did not found and concentrate the Universe in an atom. "Everything which surpasses the size of an atom is a super-fluous and useless existence."[2] Why are there so many men? Why not but one? Why is a single tone not a symphony? The end of the tree is its fruit. Why, then, the leaves, the

[1] *La Réligion*, p. 178. [2] Ibid., p. 179

trunk, the branches, the roots? If the end of the man is to be a man, why is he first an embryo, then a baby, then a boy, then a youth? "Truly, if one extend this point of view to all teleological ideas, one arrives at this conclusion, that all sensible and material life is pure superfluity, useless waste, and that the best would be that there should be nothing; for in the nothing would there be unity, and thus all inutility and all superfluity would disappear."[1]

Nature, it is on the other hand replied, is greedy for life. How does this fit in with the existence of tremendous uninhabited and vacuous spaces? Easily. The creative penchant of nature is at the same time a destructive penchant. The birth of one is the death of another. The conservation of matter and of energy thus reposes on the destruction of forms of matter and of energy. That is why these are called laws of conservation, not laws of augmentation or aggrandizement. Nature is not as avid of life as are those individuals who use this dictum to try to prove that their limited lives are unlimited. If it were, it would have divided and separated life, giving a particular world to each species of plant and of animal; or it might have given to each individual a separate world as his own property. Such a cosmic organization certainly would more nearly conform to man's end than that which exists, and in which are piled up one upon another our mutually-devouring lives. An isolated and independent man, inhabiting a world all his own, might never die. For in such a world there would be all unity and no difference. But such is not our world. Our world is quite different, in which the union and connections of men —the social contract, if you will—are the basis of all

[1] *La Réligion*, p. 180.

language, consequently of all thought,* and also of death. "For man only dies by man; he only exists and lives by his separation and essential liaison with others."[1]

The argument against the locus of the hereafter being in the stars concludes by showing that if that were true, life would have to continue without interruption everywhere. Were it not so, the plant which dies on earth would have to grow on from its immediate pre-death form in Saturn. Dying there, it would have to grow on in its pre-Saturn-death form in Uranus, and so on for ever, piteously dwarfing Jack the Giantkiller's beanstalk. But this is prohibited us by our earlier analysis. Celestial periods can contain no form different from those terrestrial, for with each change of form a void, a lucuna would be created that would have to be filled—if we are to believe that the laws of conservation of energy and matter are real, that a given quantity of life on any planet will continue. Whence would this be filled? Not from another planet, for even if the fantastic process we have outlined above were to operate in rotation, babies would no longer be born, but physical and intellectual giants, full grown, would step on to the earthly scene to overflow the gaps left by men's deaths. As the Arkansas pastor prayed when his invocations for relief from drought had been answered by a flood, "However, Lord, this is ridiculous."

It is not only the refutation of this sort of teleology which is important in the above, but also the implicit or

* cf. Briffault, "Language is not, as at one time supposed, the device invented by a transcendent intellect to achieve self-utterance, but the source whence that intellect itself has sprung into being." Quoted by Calverton, *The Passing of the Gods*, New York, 1934, p. 10.

[1] *La Réligion*, p. 181.

indirect refutation both of the argument from design, the creation of the world *ex nihilo,* and all types of literal immortalist eschatology in general. For, be it remembered, this argument is based upon the metaphysical presupposition of the Hegelian Idea.

We have touched briefly upon the role of limitation in affairs cosmic. This point is here deserving of brief expatiation.

Everything which exists is, in one way or another, limited. Existence and limitation might, indeed, be considered synonymous terms. Only nothingness is without limits. "Against the void there is only one possible arm, and this arm is limitation."[1] Limitation for each thing is its support and definition; it is not an exterior thing, like the fence around a pasture; it is the centre of being. Everything in nature is what it is not by virtue of that of which it is composed, but rather by the peculiar determination of undefined matter in it, by the particular mode of aggregation of its elements—it is just this that gives importance to chemistry—by its relation to the things which it is not.* The essence, the very life of beings is in consequence measure, form, species, or law. We have discussed a white horse before. The constituent chemistry of this horse, indiscriminately spattered over the Universe, is in no intelligible sense the horse. What defines the animal—his horseness, if you will—is his size, his shape, his construction, the relations of his tail, his mane, his head, his fetlocks,

[1] Ibid., p. 183.

* A noted comic-strip character, Popeye, catches up this thought more succinctly than many a professional philosopher by his oft-repeated "I yam what I yam because I yam not what I yam not."

even his peculiar appetites and his gait. What is this form if not limitation and measure?

Human life also has a necessary limit, but for which the human personality in its distinctive form would not exist. Because of the limitations of his respiratory apparatus man is not a salmon, just as the salmon is not a man because he has gills instead of a nose. Just as the aqueous environment in which the salmon dwells makes him what he is, so the mundane environment in which we live makes us what we are. If we have any common denominator it is the earth, which is indeed a determined measure, but *within* which there is—in general mathematical terms—an indenumerable, inexhaustible determination which produces and conserves all the diverse forms of life which we know on earth. It is, in a determinate sense, our ineluctable measure. "It contains species and infinite differences, and all are contained within the common measure which establishes its own nature; it follows that terrestrial nature, inasmuch as it embraces all, is the uncrossable limit of everything that lives on the earth and consequently of the life of man."[1] This being so, it must be recognized that where these indispensable conditions of life do not obtain, no human life is possible.

The preceding objection may seem like that of simply naïve empiricism. But on closer examination it will be seen that it can be overcome only by the immortalist who gives us so unconcrete, vague and amorphous a definition of the human personality that it is meaningless.*

[1] *La Réligion*, p. 186. Feuerbach's use of the word *infinite* is not, of course, here mathematically correct. In defence it can only be said that, with the still highly incomplete knowledge of man about his world, it might be called humanly correct.

* For our part, we must maintain, until we investigate the matter further, that whatever definition of the soul or personality be proposed,

Another point. If man were to accomplish his real destiny only in another life, on this earth there would be no philosophy and no science. Instead of the various abstract ideas, or powers of thought, which we now have in our brains, those whom Feuerbach calls "our celestial brothers" would be the inhabitants. "Instead of mathematics, logic, or metaphysics, we would have ever-present in our minds the most exact portraits of those beings we are going to be called upon to resemble one day,"[1] just as children have images of their future selves in their day-dreams. These portraits of our future selves—if we were to be what the immortalists tell us—would intrude themselves before our thoughts because they are qualitatively different and of a higher order than the images and abstractions which are now in our brains. Our future selves would be closer to us than thoughts and ideas, not being abstract being, but sensible and spiritual beings which alone would express the essence of the imagination. These being dominant, our external life would have less than the reality of a dream. But the preceding is, of course, not so; man's very power of objectivating himself, of getting out and beyond the world of the senses and to the life of the reason is itself a negation of this chimera. This in itself is the "proof in fact that our terrestrial existence is our last existence, our manner of being the most perfect, the most sublime."[2] For from the moment we are

it must at least contain the faculty of memory or consciousness of self-identity. Without this faculty it cannot be maintained that whatever personality-projection the immortalist conjures up is really a given individual's immortal soul. Without recognition, we have no witness that this projection is not a shade—or a real being, for that matter—which has no relation whatsoever to the earthly individual. In short, if Napoleon's immortal soul does not know that it is Napoleon, we have no right to say that it is, even though saying so may make us more comfortable.

[1] *La Réligion*, p. 186.   [2] Ibid., p. 187.

able to lift ourselves above our sensible life we have no need of counterposing ourselves to more perfect beings in order to arrive in mind at the conception of infinite being.

It is nature's limits which make thought possible. "If the nature of the earth had not here below its entire fulfilment, if it did not develop all the possible forms with which it clothes the beings which it produces ceaselessly, if in creating man it had not cried: 'Thus far and no further!' Well! man would not think. Thought is the expression of satiety, of satisfaction, of complete perfection; through it the last seal is placed on the work of life; it is the supreme, uncrossable frontier of thinking beings. Thus the sublimest life is that of religion, science, and art. That is the life above transient life, the life above death."[1]

We may be permitted to pause here to note the thorough-going Hegelianism of the preceding passage. To Hegel art and religion were but varying forms of the sentimental or feeling aspect of the Idea,[2] itself the metaphysical alpha and omega, the beginning and end of the dialectic. But—and here is the important difference—Hegel nowhere uses this construction explicitly to investigate literal transcendentalist eschatology. Only in very general, but not in specific, terms is he a pantheist. Only in very general, but not in specific, terms does his system permit a highly impersonal immortality. Hegel is interested in the problem of immortality only in so far as it helps him understand and clarify the central role of the Idea. Feuerbach, on the other hand,

---

[1] *La Réligion*, pp. 187–8.

[2] cf. Hegel's *Philosophy of Religion*, translated by Speirs and Sanderson, London, 1895; section on *The Relation of the Philosophy of Religion to its Presuppositions and to the Principles of the Time*, pp. 6–48.

believes the problem to be of sufficient importance to men to deserve exhaustive direct treatment. Feuerbach's fundamental departure from Hegelianism is perhaps here better evident than at any other point. He wishes to investigate the problem from the point of view of anthropology. "The anthropological point of departure is the existence of this belief in immortality; for it the existence is the primary thing, not existence in the sense of Hegel's logic, identical with thought, but existence guaranteed by the witness of the senses."[1] Hegel, on the other hand, had stated his point of departure thusly: "In philosophy, the Highest is . . . the Absolute, the Idea; it is superfluous to go further back here."[2] And religion was for him the elevation of the Absolute *qua* Absolute to an object of sensuous contemplation.

Feuerbach is not satisfied with answering the insistent question of immortality in one vein. He preliminarily exhausts the question on an Hegelian basis, proving the fatuity of the doctrine of personal immortalism as we have seen in the preceding pages of this chapter. He then assesses the psychologically dualist position, which is the unacknowledged position held by a great number of contemporary pro-immortalist eschatologists who have been given by the findings of modern science completely to separate soul from body in order to conserve a transcendental heaven.* Feuerbach's words to them might well have been written but a week ago rather than a century ago.

---

[1] Feuerbach, op. cit., p. 303.   [2] Hegel, op. cit., p. 23.

* It is of collateral interest to note how mute on the findings of modern psychology are the immortalists who wax most enthusiastic about the findings of modern astrophysics. Cursory recapitulation of the latter appears to them to support their doctrine, while the former—tying ever tighter the bonds between soul and body—is in no wise a support to them.

"The soul," he writes, "no matter how incorporeal, is as little soul without body as the master is master without slaves, the end end without means. The relation between the soul and body is, so to speak, that between fire and combustible matter. The body is tinder, the nutritive matter of the soul. Where there is no matter there is no fire. In this sense it can be said that fire is subordinate to matter, that it is the instrument of matter; but when fire devours matter, then it is the master of matter, it is a power. Just as the fire ceases as soon as there is no more combustible material; just so the soul, when it has devoured all its body, when it is worn out and destroyed by continual usage, when there are no more elements in it against which it may show its activity, and by the destruction of which it is what it is—just so the soul dies."[1] Immateriality, then, is not a fixed attribute, as the whiteness and thickness of this paper are its permanent attributes. The soul is only immaterial in the sense that it negates and devours material. This does not mean, either, that we must accept the view that the soul is material like the clam within his shell. The soul, again in Feuerbach's words, "is pure life, pure activity, sacred and incorruptible fire. . . . But this pure activity, this soul such as it is, identical with a particular body, finishes with this body."[2] In this vein is the dualist conception disposed of.

We have mentioned that Feuerbach's own approach to the problem of immortality was anthropological.* We have briefly seen his answer to two other eschatologies. It is to

[1] Feuerbach, op. cit., pp. 195–6.   [2] *La Réligion*, p. 196.

* Feuerbach's initial answer, *Thoughts on Death and Immortality*, was, as we have seen, in an Hegelian vein. This was written in 1830. *Immortality from the Point of View of Anthropology*, chief among his later works upon the subject, was written in 1846.

his analysis of the genetic origin of the belief in immortality that we now turn. Herein we note the important difference between the Feuerbach of 1830 and the Feuerbach of the 1840's.

There is historically a subjective necessity for belief in immortality. The basis of this belief is not man's tendency toward continual perfection, as some ontologists tell us; it is, rather, man's simpler instinct of self-conservation. He does not wish to let escape from his hands that which he possesses. Fichte's contention was that we cannot love any object that we do not believe to be eternal. This is only half the truth. Man can undertake virtually nothing without attaching the idea of duration to it. Who would build a house, paint a picture, or write a book if he were not sure that the house, canvas, or manuscript would not be destroyed the next day? True, the given object might be destroyed by fire overnight, but it is on the assumption that it will not be that the creative work is undertaken. Fichte's assertion that the object of man's affection need be eternal is difficult to maintain. Only a presumptuous man would insist that his work of art will last for eternity. He will, however, envision an *indefinite* future for his work. So with human life; the feeling for immortality is not for life eternal but for life indefinitely long.

This is particularly true, asserts Feuerbach, in man's early life. At sunrise we would be unhappily shocked if we knew that the sun were to set immediately without giving us an opportunity to perform our day's work. By late afternoon, on the other hand, we are ready for sunset. The content of the day has conditioned our mode of looking at things, of thinking, specifically, about sunset. There is a distinction, then, between what Feuerbach calls the veritable end and an imaginary end. The content of life prepares us for the former; it is only the latter which goes against the psychological grain.

Immortality is an imaginative desire which has its origin in the fact that, by comparison with time, the idea of a relatively eternal life is a felt need of man's. But here man contradicts, in large measure, reality. Life is, in fact, long; but in the imagination it appears to be short. This is especially so in middle and old age. The child thinks it a long time between school holidays. His parents think life short. But the child is right. "Why? Because we no longer regard the past as our property, and our spent existence is worth as much as nothing. We make of the time in our lives what the miser makes with his treasure; when his coffers are filled with gold and silver he still believes he has nothing. I can always have much more in imagination than I really have; reality always lags far behind."[1] But this is obviously a false way of looking at things. Has the two-thirds of his dinner that a man has eaten thereby ceased to be his dinner in any save, perhaps, a chemical sense? When the traveller from London to Paris reaches Dieppe, has the channel crossing which he has just made ceased to be part of his journey only because he has already accomplished it? Obviously not. Yet it is true, as regards the problem of human life, that many men think in this fashion. But then, if it were true—i.e. that the man of seventy-nine destined to die at eighty "lives" but one year—then if man should live thousands of years he would naught gain thereby. Because, even at the ripe old age of six million, Mr. Meta-

[1] *The Essence of Christianity*, p. 238.

methuselah might expect to die at six million and one, and thus the same problem of feeling life limited would arise. "Just as, by the nature of intellectual abstraction, we abbreviate and generalize everything, in concentrating in a single image or a single idea the real world, leaving aside its particularities and its infinite diversities;—so by our imaginations do we concentrate in a single fugitive instant our entire life with its immense riches, its long duration,* and often its insupportable boredom, and thereby we are obliged to enlarge this imaginary brevity by means of an imaginary duration also."[1]

Another important commentary here stems from the idea of growth. When man arrives at his natural death he does not die as a lad or man, but as an old man. "Death does not enter my house by breaking down the door; it has its reasons for coming in; it announces and introduces itself."[2] Between the individual and death there is an important mediator, life, the progress and process of life. Each new degree of life is the death of that which preceded it. The soul of man's infance or his youth has not gone to God or to heaven or to Neptune; it exists no more than does the man when he has ceased to live. Certain eschatologists, denying the above, say that the child's soul grows up and becomes the man's. We cannot, however, accept this soul definition, hypostatized to suit the exigencies of its applications to be. The child only regards as true life his own life. The personality of the youth is to him the only true

* To a fly, or even to a dog, man's life must seem—if either animal could reflect upon the matter—a practical eternity; just as a mythical life of, say, nine hundred years seems a practical eternity to us.

[1] *The Essence of Christianity*, p. 238.   [2] Ibid., p. 239.

personality; he is above childish things on the one hand and is proud of his strength and vigour to the contempt of mature manhood on the other. "Take from the child his toys, and this destruction of his manner of self-expression will be as terrible to him as death to you. However, there comes a moment when the young man denies his infance and the man his youth. That which was all for them now is nothing. If we find it natural that infance and youth pass away, why worry because we will finally die?"[1]

Feuerbach's answer to the latter question is simply that man's egoism keeps him from admitting the natural consequences of the foregoing, just as it hinders him from profiting in his own time by the lessons of history. Where man's egoism commences, there the laws of logic lose all value.

Whence, anthropologically, comes the idea of life after death? It is, from the point of view of its psychological genesis, nothing more than the idea of man's own future, transformed by man into a more perfect state; just as he transforms into a spiritual being, different from nature, the laws of nature. It is in this way that the life after death is by us represented as much better than our present lives. We are sensibly aware of the evils of the present life; not so of the evils of a future life. For the future life is uniquely dependent on our fantasy or our wishes; for it everything is possible. "The beggar is a millionaire, the corporal emperor, the man God."[2] And here we must answer the ontologists who tell us that the fact that man has the idea of immortality is itself a proof of the necessity and existence of immortality. The medieval monk Gaunilo had answered

[1] *The Essence of Christianity*, p. 239.   [2] Ibid., p. 241.

this argument, in another connection, by asserting that he had an idea of a perfect island at a given location. The idea did not, however, prove the existence of the island, as empirical investigation could testify. To Feuerbach the same argument proves the existence of immortality only to "whoever makes his imagination the measure of what is and what ought to be."[1] This argument has value, in short —and here Feuerbach takes an intransigeant stand against his idealist philosophical forbears—only for "whoever derives the world from a thought, from a word, from a spirit."[2] For such a metaphysics there exists not the slightest difficulty in constructing future worlds on a simple concept of intelligence. But for he who finds neither in faith nor in speculation the power to work miracles, the idea of immortality serves only to prove and to express the activity of the imagination. "I can," concludes Feuerbach, "without encountering any obstacle, extend my life thoughout all time; but this lack of limitation proves precisely that it is an imaginary life."[3]

The fundamental conclusion which we can draw from the anthropological investigation into the belief in immortality is this: The idea stems from man's instinct for self-conservation and his idea of his own future, unconsciously transformed—just as is man's God—into objectivity. The concrete idea of the celestial future commences when man feels himself really limited by the narrowness of space and the determination of time. Conversely, when man's purview becomes greater, as soon as the practical infinitude of his

---

[1] *The Essence of Christianity*, p. 241.
[2] Ibid., p. 241.
[3] Ibid., p. 242.

possible world becomes patent to him,* he puts in place of the future life the present life, adjoining to it the memory of the past and the hope of the historic future. He substitutes "in place of the other world the rest of the real world until then unknown by him. The other world is only truly realized by civilization. Civilization causes the limits imposed by time and space to disappear, elevates us above the present, transports us into times far removed, renders us capable of living back the thousands of years which were for us the absence of all action, knowledge, and existence; and permits us to know, by analogy and in advance, future centuries in which we will live no longer."[1]

Up to this point we have been discussing immortality in general. A few observations on immortality from the point of view of the Christian heaven are now in order.

"The doctrine of immortality," says Feuerbach, "is the final doctrine of religion; its testament, in which it declares its last wishes."[2] And here, he adds, the human character of religion is patently revealed. As we have previously noted, man, in the development of religion, concerns himself with the existence of a being which theologically has become a being other than himself. In the doctrine of immortality, however, the religious soul considers openly its own existence. Elsewhere in religion man tends to make his own existence dependent upon the existence of God; here he makes the reality of God dependent upon his own reality. The Apostle Paul drew the conclusion that if we do not

* This practical infinitude is well expressed by the oft-quoted saying, "The more you know, the more you find out there is to know."

[1] *The Essence of Christianity*, p. 247.

[2] Ibid., p. 174.

rise again, then Christ is not risen.* If Christ is not risen, God is not God. Thus God and heaven become in a large measure identical in Christianity. The whole problem therefore assumes critical proportions in Christianity. For the emphasis upon personal immortality is one of the most characteristic of Christian doctrines. Christianity is, it might be said, unique among religions in having the idea of personal immortality fundamental to the structure of the religion itself. In other religions the doctrine of immortality is rather an appendix to the religion itself. The major presumptions of the theology do not stand or fall as its eschatology stands or falls.

One of the fundamental tenets of orthodox Christian theology is that the unwedded or ascetic life is the direct way to the heavenly, immortal life; heaven is life largely liberated from the essential conditions of the species. Thus heavenly life, it is assumed, is sexless, supernatural, and wholly subjective. A direct corollary, therefore, of the Christian doctrine of personal immortality is the belief that

* An interesting commentary on this notion is afforded in a letter to Charles Kingsley written by the eminent biologist Thomas Huxley: "As I stood beside the coffin of my little son the other day, with my mind bent on anything but disputation, the officiating minister read, as a part of his duty, the words, 'If the dead rise not again, let us eat and drink, for tomorrow we die.' I cannot tell you how inexpressibly they shocked me. I could have laughed with scorn. What! Because I am face to face with irreparable loss, because I have given back to the source from which it came the cause of a great happiness, still retaining through all my life the blessings which have sprung and will spring from that cause, I am to renounce my manhood, and, howling, grovel in bestiality? Why, the very apes know better, and if you shoot their young, the poor brutes grieve their grief out and do not immediately seek distraction in a gorge." Huxley, *Life and Letters of Thos. H. Huxley*, New York, 1900, vol. i, p. 237.

difference of sex is only an external, non-fundamental adjunct of individuality. The essence of the individual is, then, sexless and independently complete. But this belief robs man of his natural relation to the whole of the world. He who belongs to no sex belongs to no species, and he who belongs to no species belongs only to himself. Therefore the man who lives in the consciousness of his species (and what man, even among Biblical characters, has not?) can conceive no life in which the life of the species is abolished. The sexless individual, the heavenly spirit, is an agreeable figment of the imagination, but he is no man's immortal self; he is another self. And obviously we are not personally immortal if we are represented in the hereafter by other selves.

In line with our analysis of the essence of Christianity, what can we say, in addition to what we have already said about immortality, about Christian immortality? As God is nothing else than the nature of man purified from that which to the human individual appears, whether in feeling or in thought, a limitation; "so the future life is nothing else than the present life freed from that which appears a limitation or an evil."[1] The future life is the conception of freedom from the limits which circumscribe the feeling of self. The only difference between the course of religion and that of natural man is that the former arrives by a detour at the point to which the latter goes directly. The natural man lives in harmony with himself and is satisfied. In religion man separates himself from himself; he unconsciously negates himself and then, aware of his inner disunion, consciously recreates that union on a different

[1] *The Essence of Christianity*, p. 181.

level in a glorified form. He negates this life, but only in the end to posit it again in the future life, which is this life once lost but refound. "The religious man renounces the joys of this world but only that he may win in return the joys of heaven; or rather he renounces them because he is already in the ideal possession of heavenly joys; and the joys of heaven are the same as those of earth, only that they are freed from the limits and the contrarieties of this life. Religion thus arrives, though by a circuit, at the very goal, the goal of joy, towards which the natural man hastens in a direct line."[1] The future life is but an embellishment of the present life, contemplated through the imagination, purified of certain of the grosser aspects of this life. Religion has a natural affinity for this conception because religion itself lives in images or symbols, sacrificing the thing itself to the image. The future life is the present, seen through the spectacles of imagery and symbolism peculiar to religion.

So much for the substance of the Feuerbachian arguments with relation to immortality. If they seem to be, in a certain sense, negative, it is because Feuerbach considered it necessary to clear away considerable underbrush of false and misleading conceptions. He was himself aware of this negative aspect of his work, writing as a supplementary remark to his *Thoughts on Death and Immortality* the following later published sentences: "The principal reproach which has been made with reference to these thoughts on death and immortality is that they are absolutely negative, that they destroy, wipe out personality. This reproach is thoroughly superficial. If I prove to a man that he is not in reality what he believes to be in imagination, I am

[1] *The Essence of Christianity*, p. 182.

certainly negative toward him; I do harm to him; I take away his illusion. But I am only negative toward his imagined, not his real, self."[1]

Despite the argumentative aspect of the work as outlined in the preceding pages of this chapter, there emerges a not too unsystematic positive side. Let us recapitulate in stating the position on this more positive side.

Death has a physical cause, a psychological origin, a metaphysical reason, and a positive moral value.* We shall briefly discuss these *seriatim*. First of all, death has a physical cause; immortality would be the negation of all we know about nature. Every living thing, animal or plant, changes incessantly by the very fact of living;† the continual history of successive deaths is what we call life. The soul and body, as we have seen, are inseparably linked. To call the soul thought, liberty, will, or self-consciousness is properly the work of the human faculty known as abstraction; but the separation of the soul and body is not material; it is spiritual. To believe that this abstract distinction possesses concrete reality is to be victim of an hallucination.

Secondly, death has a psychological origin. The mind, the conscience are universal. In thinking, in Hegelian terms, man absorbs himself in the Idea. Man's existence is reduced in his essence. Universal conscience is light; individuals are

---

[1] Feuerbach, *Thoughts on Death and Immortality*, edited and translated by J. Roy, p. 291.

* These categories, in a different order and in a somewhat different sense, are delineated by Lévy, op. cit., chap. iii.

† cf. Epikuros, "For the deepest anxieties of the human heart arise from this, that we regard these earthly things as abiding and satisfying, and so we must tremble at all the changes which nevertheless occur. But he who regards change in things as necessarily inherent in their very existence is obviously freer from this error."

colours which come only through refraction. Awareness belongs to all humanity; it existed before any individual emerged, and it exists after he ceases to be. The function of man, imposed on him by his instinct or bent, gives the individual his right to life. When his human task is finished, man disappears; his internal end both opens and closes man's career. Another life, without end and without vocation, would be either just a game, or superfluous, or both. We survive in history if we have truly lived; we will for ever occupy in the memory of men the place that we have really won and occupied. "Heaven is the glory; hell, the malediction of posterity."[1] Death, then, destroys in us only that part of us which ought to perish, the finite, loveless being. This is the part of man which is not assimilable in humanity, which cannot survive in its living memory. Thus death is the negation of a negation. The quantity of life does not count; only the quality or content is important. True immortality can be seized in this life; each moment can potentially have infinite value. Eternity, then, is a meaningful term when applied to human life. It is force, energy, act.

Thirdly, death has a metaphysical reason. At the time when Feuerbach wrote his *Thoughts on Death and Immortality* he was, as we have observed earlier in the chapter, still an Hegelian. God to him was mind or spirit, i.e. He was simultaneously soul and conscience, nature and the individual, subject and object. Thus He was established as both the principle and end of existence; He was not only the absolute Self, but also an absolute non-Self; that is, everything outside the individual which limits and deter-

[1] Lévy, op. cit., p. 64.

mines him. Individual death, then, presupposes an eternal and general supersensible death, God. The Infinite is immanent—this was the point of repair of Hegel's pantheism —and it is this infinity that causes the breaking up of the various transient forms of the finite. The individual, in this view, dies precisely because he is not capable of conserving in the present that which he seeks to acquire in the future. Death does not stem from a lack, but from an excess.

Fourthly, death has a positive moral value. To be moral is to be unselfish, to live for one another, to love, to deny one's egoistic self. But death, as we have established in discussing its psychological origin, is nothing but the natural negation of man; it is thus the act by which nature submits itself, so to speak, to the moral will or principle. Love would not be perfect without death. "In loving, thou judgest thyself worthy of death; nature only executes thy end; death is thus a supreme act of liberty."[1] Death is the achievement of man's internal emancipation. It is not after its coming that we should try to triumph over it. We should await it joyfully and positively as a last deliverance.

*　　*　　*　　*　　*

So much for the "systematic" aspect of Feuerbach's philosophy of immortality. It is in comparing it with one of the most thoroughgoing of modern works* on the problem that its adequacies and inadequacies best stand out.

At the present time men speak of immortality in several senses. This is probably true in considerable measure, because the old ground of personal immortality has become

[1] Lévy, op. cit., p. 61.
* Lamont, *The Illusion of Immortality*, London, 1936.

less and less tenable for some of the reasons set forth earlier in the chapter. In trying to conserve some notion of immortality, then, eschatologists have taken refuge behind the irrefutable ideas of chemical immortality (the chemical constituents of the human body, returning to the earth, become a part of some future life), the idea of biological immortality (man is immortal through the passage of his seed to his children, thence to his grandchildren, thence to his great grandchildren, and so on), and the idea of influential immortality (man's influence is felt on the world after his death through his good works: through the buildings he may build, the symphonies he may write, or, more abstractly, the good deeds which he may do to his fellow men, who catching the same spirit, do good deeds to their fellow men, and so on).* This latter is, by and large, the positive conception proclaimed by Feuerbach.

None can deny the truth of any of the three preceding conceptions of immortality. We believe in immortality in this sense. But this, on which there is general agreement, is not the issue. The issue is "immortality as signifying the continuation of the individual personality after death . . . that is the meaning of immortality that has so moved mankind in every age and every place."[1] The foregoing is implicit in what Feuerbach writes, but it is with him nowhere as clearly stated as the above.†

---

* This conception has been vigorously and effectively popularized through some of the writings of Dr. Lloyd C. Douglas, particularly in his novel, *The Magnificent Obsession.*

[1] Lamont, loc. cit., p. 24.

† Partly, probably, because these alternative conceptions of immortality were not as widespread in his day as at present; "immortality" always meant "personal immortality" a century ago.

Feuerbach was not, obviously, in a position to assess the verdict of science in the way in which we can assess that verdict to-day. His argument for the unity of the soul and body was, however, Aristotelian—i.e. the soul is a function of the body—and as such it is completely in accord with the major generalizations of modern psychology. We may sum up the position, first of all, from the point of view of biology and physiology. "For the individual comes out of the germ-plasm and does and lives and at length dies for the sake of life. It is a bit of the germ-plasm which has arisen and broken away, in order to see and feel life instead of just blindly and mechanically multiplying. Like Faust it has sold its immortality in order to live more abundantly."[1] Discussing the question from the point of view of modern medicine, we have additional data which are arresting. Typical is the following:

Eschatologists of the psychological dualist persuasion insist that upon death the soul leaves the body and hies itself heavenward. Thus a certain American wrote some years ago about his brief experience in the hereafter at a time when he alleges he was ill. It was his contention that his earthly body was so near death that his soul had already fled and gone to heaven, only to be recalled when his body took a turn for the better. In recent years considerable progress has been made by medicine in the use of the "artificial heart." People whose hearts have stopped beating for some minutes (and thus are technically dead) have been revived by means of this mechanical device or by means of heart injections. None of the people who have undergone

[1] H. G. Wells, Julian Huxley, G. P. Wells, *The Science of Life*, New York, 1931, p. 551; quoted by Lamont, op. cit., p. 66.

this experience of death and subsequent revivification have reported anything save a period of total blankness during the lifeless interim. Where, immortalists, were their souls during this period?

Numerous other indices of this nature are adduced in support of the general position. The verdict of science—biological, physiological, psychological, and medical—"is clearly in favour of that monistic psychology which sees man as an inseparable oneness of personality and body. Implicit in this psychology is a denial, and indeed a disproof, of the idea of immortality. . . . All in all, therefore, the results of science, coupled with our earlier analysis of various immortality ideas, set up a very powerful case in support of our thesis that immortality is an illusion."[1] As far, then, as this part of Lamont's analysis can be connected to Feuerbach's, we can say that the rapport is one of support. The theses are mutually sustaining of the dictum contained in the major premise of that most famous of Aristotelian syllogisms, "Man is Mortal."

Neither Feuerbach nor Lamont discusses the problem from the point of view of the history of philosophy in any great detail. Feuerbach did, in his first work, survey the field in examining the doctrines of Aristotle, Averroes, and Hegel. Thereafter he strikes out on his own, making only passing direct references to the classical arguments. Lamont, too, surveys the problem in discussing the historical beliefs and then passing on to the scientific and logical position, giving only occasional direct treatment to the traditional arguments as they are contained in the systems of philosophy. About this two things can be said. First, an

[1] Lamont, op. cit., p. 112.

exhaustive direct survey of the problem touches, in greater or less detail, the arguments of the systems and deals with the whole problem more intelligibly than it can be discussed from the point of view of the systems taken separately, unless one discuss the problem solely as it has appeared to the philosopher rather than to the man on the street. Secondly, for the very reason that the question of personal immortality is often at the apex of a system, it cannot generally be touched without demolition of the entire system. If there be any exception to the latter, it is Feuerbach's initial treatment of the problem in exclusively Hegelian terms. But even then it must be acknowledged that implicit denial of immortality was in Hegelianism proper.

One argument, however, which is relatively universal is the Kantian ethical argument. Feuerbach touches it implicitly; Lamont touches it explicitly. It is worth following his analysis here.

Kant, it will be remembered, established immortality of the soul as a postulate of the practical reason.* In so far as any of the Kantian postulates were truly derived, this postulate was derived from the premise of the inherent worth of the human personality. The latter had been established as basis for the Kantian ethic: Men are ends, not means.† The highest good for men consists in the union of virtue and happiness. The latter is attainable in this world, but the former, virtue, is strictly attainable "only in an

* cf. Kant, *Critique of Practical Reason*, Book II, chap. ii.
† cf. Kant's "So act as to treat humanity, whether in thine own person or that of any other, always as an end withal, and never as a means only."——*Metaphysic of Morality.*

infinite progress toward harmony with the moral law. . . .
This infinite progress is possible only if we presuppose that
the existence of a rational being is prolonged to infinity,
and that he retains his personality for all time."[1] Immortality
is thus bound up with the one other thing, besides the
starry heavens above, which filled Kant with awe, the moral
law. The argument continues as a variant of the ontological
argument for the existence of God. In order for immortality
to be consummated, a God with the will and ability to
realize it must exist. For it is incompatible with the definition
of divine Being to believe that his creatures should be
unable to secure the happiness which their just-defined
nature demands. In short, according to this argument, men's
moral aspirations are so perfect, so lofty, so in harmony
with the structure of the noumenal world, that there must
be an immortality to permit of their self-realization. Thus,
in the last analysis, immortality makes God, rather than
God making immortality.

In this, "Kant takes what had been an accepted and
usually unquestioned part of the *description* of immortality,
namely, its ethical content, and turns it, appending certain
qualifications of his own, into an *argument* for immortality.
Here we see an excellent example of how the reasons offered
to make an idea acceptable are inextricably bound up in a
constant interaction with the content of the idea itself."[2]

Analysis of the preceding idea is important both because
of the frequency with which it appears in the philosophical
arguments, and also because, unchallenged, it gives all sorts

---

[1] *Critique of Practical Reason*, Book II, chap. ii, quoted by Lamont,
op. cit., p. 143.

[2] Lamont, op. cit., p. 144.

of wish-fulfilment metaphysical status. An analogous type of fulfilment, instinct-fulfilment, is at the core of another argument for personal immortality. Feuerbach stressed that the instinct for self-conservation was, anthropologically speaking, the root of all immortality ideas. Certain immortalists in his day were prone to insist that until instinct could be adequately defined, it was impossible to deny that man's instinct for self-conservation was not the seed of immortality itself. Lamont points out that the immortalists should be consistent here; if they say that man's instinct to live happily after death is proof of heaven, what corresponding instinct have we as proof of hell? Who has "a natural desire for the possibility of everlasting torments for either oneself or one's fellow-men"?[1]

Implicit in these fulfilment ideas, which are so often used as bases for personal immortalism arguments, is an important metaphysical principle. Feuerbach referred to it in observing that the immortalist variant of the ontological argument is meaningful only to those who derive the world from a thought, from a word, from a spirit. Regardless of the particular argument invoked, the procedure is approximately the same as Kant's in drawing the immortality rabbit out of the moral law's silk hat. Lamont sums up the situation thusly: "What all of them (immortalists) do is to assume that what man considers supremely good or ethical or desirable should and does constitute one of the fundamental traits of existence as such. . . . For, if the universe-as-a-whole is to be conceived as caring sufficiently for human personalities to make them immortal . . . then it must be a universe at the very core of which exists a full

[1] Lamont, op. cit., p. 153.

appreciation of human standards. This means that goodness, justice, rationality, purpose, and so on must be among the ultimate metaphysical aspects of existence, characteristics of the cosmos at large instead of existent or potential attributes of nature in some relative capacity."[1]

From this arise such confusions as that about duration. We have already considered the natural way in which men come to attach certain indefinite durational standards to their activity. But when these standards are objectivated— just as are men's gods—when they receive metaphysical status, their indefinite duration automatically becomes eternity.* We have observed how, in Feuerbach's analysis, unlimited duration would mean the end of all sensation. In addition, it is important to criticize the immortalist's assumption, based upon the just-noted illicit metaphysical principle, that value and duration are akin; that that which is not eternal is not intrinsically to be valued. Aristotle gave a classic answer to this assumption when he observed that "a good will not be more good if it is eternal, since a white thing which lasts for a long time is not whiter than that which lasts a single day."[2] And a trenchant complement is afforded by Mumford's "The notion that a quantitative existence in time is a necessary measure of worth, without which life is a blank, is a notion that occurs only when life is a blank anyway."[3] This point, indeed, would scarcely be

---

[1] Lamont, op. cit., p. 158.

* It must be observed here that Lamont does not explain whence comes the assignment to objects of metaphysical status. He simply accepts it as a datum. But is it not just the comprehension of how this transition occurs that is at the heart of our problem?

[2] Aristotle, *Nichomachean Ethics*, Book I, chap. iv.

[3] Quoted by Lamont, op. cit., p. 159.

worth mentioning were it not for the fact that it is ridden so often and so hard by modern defenders of personal immortality. The quality of life is, of course, completely separable from its quantity. Some of the greatest spirits the world has ever known have died the youngest.

We have mentioned the Kantian assertion that infinite time is necessary for the realization of the union of virtue and happiness. A variant of this is the oft-stated theological argument that men's souls must continue to be perfected, and that immortality is therefore necessary. One may be pardoned for querying in this connection about the fate of the perfect souls which have existed on earth, and are now canonized. How about the soul of a Christ? Perfected, what is its reason for immortality? Or, returning to Kant, if an earthly Utopia were established, would there still be necessity for immortality? Here we arrive at the important social aspect of the problem, touched upon by Lamont.

One of the chief reasons for the persistence of immortality ideas has been the earthly social situation. Institutional religion, frequently unable to answer the cry for bread, has given men the stone of immortality. The disinherited have been, psychologically, all too ready to revel in dreams about the beatitude of a future life in which social and economic equality would be a fact. Princes of privilege have been quick to seize upon this in order to turn the eyes of the exploited toward the pearly gates and away from the actual world, the wrongs of which might be righted by them should they face their social situation more frankly. It was this fact which caused Marx to comment caustically: "The mortgage held by the peasants on the heavenly estates guarantees the mortgage held by the bourgeoisie on the peasant estates."[1] Such social phenomena as ill-health and premature death* on the part of working people unable to afford medical and other safeguards, devastating wars, crime, and the like are increasingly traceable to class-economic roots. It is this fact which causes Lamont to conclude that ". . . a drastic change in the economic and social system, making the world a safer and saner place to live in, would have far-reaching effects on the extent and strength of belief in a hereafter. A more rational social order would, in my opinion, quickly result in a sweeping decline in the influence of immortality ideas."[2]

To a considerable extent the agreements and differences between the Feuerbachian and present positions have been made clear in the foregoing. To state it more explicitly: Feuerbach's analysis is admittedly individualist; he shows clearly how individuals become convinced, through certain unrecognized intellectual and emotional operations of their own, of the fact of a future life, and why this concept is false. Not only this. He demonstrates, not too systematically but none the less lucidly, the positive value of anti-immortalism in his ethic of love. He presents an alternative conception of immortality which is meaningful in a humanist sense, borrowed in part from Aristotle and in part from Averroes. And he chases away many of the ghosts which have made small boys want to whistle when walking through graveyards.

Lamont has stated the position in clear terms. He has

---

[1] Marx, *The Class Struggle in France*, New York, 1924, p. 112.

* For it is *premature* death, according to the already-examined position of Feuerbach, which robs the individual of the mediating influence of the content of a full life, and thus makes him particularly susceptible to immortality ideas.   [2] Lamont, op. cit., p. 204.

adduced the best of modern evidence, and has shown us the problem—which Feuerbach did not—in its social context. He does not, however, show us the inner operation of human fetishism,* but rather accepts the whole doctrine as an illusion which men have ignorantly acquired, which has been implemented by the unprogressive forces in society, and which will become less potent and possibly vanish as our social world becomes more reasonably organized.

Feuerbach, on the other hand, implies that simple realization by man of his heretofore unrecognized psychological make-up is sufficient. Late in 1848 he terminated his lectures on the *Essence of Religion* in Heidelberg in these words: "I hope that my auditors will be converted, that they may henceforth be no longer friends of God but friends of men, no longer believers but thinkers, no longer devotees who pray but workers who work, no longer candidates for the hereafter but students of the here below, no longer Christians who, according to their confession and their own avowal, are half angels and half beasts, but men, entirely men."[1]

It is not our intention here to engage in a socio-methodological discussion on these two types of approach. The inadequacies of Feuerbach's social point of view will become clearer as we subsequently discuss his relations with Marx. What is important is to observe Feuerbach's analysis in some detail—as Marx did, and as many present-day Marxists do not—in order to broaden our understanding and to fill up the lacuna which, we submit, exists in the otherwise comprehensive modern analysis which we have considered.

* Indeed, he makes only passing reference to Feuerbach.
[1] Quoted by Lévy, op. cit., pp. 157–8.

Finally, it is our contention that we have both directly and comparatively proved that personal immortality—in so far as the subject can be exhausted (and we maintain it can) within the domain of presuppositionless reason—is an illusion. The conclusion is in no sense a disappointing one; quite the contrary. In the words of Feuerbach, "Nature is to me a mother; I can feel myself redescend without inquietude into the bosom of the earth; I wish to be interred completely in this earth which is my native earth. *Ubi patria, ibi bene.* To wish to emigrate into another world is to desert. What matter if our canton is poor? The simple fruits of my village are better than the most exotic figs; I prefer my black bread to the delicate biscuits which would be served to me in your celestial palaces. Achilles, the Greek hero, preferred to be a labourer on earth than king in the kingdom of shadows. I do not need to be consoled about my death; I do not wish to be consoled about the death of others. Grief is sacred to me; your consolations are impious. . . ."[1]

[1] Quoted by Lévy, op. cit., p. 26.

Chapter IV

FEUERBACH AND GERMAN
LITERATURE

No treatment, no matter how cursory, of the philosophy
of Feuerbach would be complete without reference to the
role which Feuerbach has played in the history of German
literature. This role was not without significance in the
domains of philosophy and politics, for the influence of
the poets on their milieu also conditioned perceptibly the
insights of the philosophers and the doctrines of the politicians. The relation between literature and politico-philo-
sophy was thus one of interaction. No study of Marx, for
example, would be complete without mention of Heine, just
as no study of Heine would be complete without mention
of Marx.

The relation of Feuerbach to nineteenth-century German
literature would itself be a matter for at least one book.
For few indeed were the writers in whose work cannot
be found traces of attraction to, or repulsion from, Feuerbachianism. This influence, to be true, is also found in the
domain of the natural sciences—through Moleschott, and,
to a lesser extent, Karl Vogt—and in the writings on
aesthetics of Hermann Hettner. We shall, however, confine
ourselves here to Feuerbach's relation to three men, the

revolutionary poet Herwegh, the realist poet and novelist Gottfried Keller, and Richard Wagner.* For in these are important aspects of Feuerbach's philosophy most clearly illustrated. Herwegh will be the first of these to occupy our attention.

The admiration of Herwegh for Feuerbach was reciprocal. In a letter of Feuerbach's to Kriege, in 1845, we read: "I find in him (Herwegh) a kindred spirit. He is free, grave, and gay—communist as am I, at heart, but not in form. He is in no wise the professional orthodox, literal, absolutist communist. In his communism everything is noble; nothing is common. For, alas! differences in human nature manifest themselves here as elsewhere."[1] Herwegh, on his part, was frank to acknowledge Feuerbach's influence over him. In his earlier writings, he seems to have been to some extent a mixture of Hegelian and Platonist. Thus we read, in a passage devoted to the necessary progress of ideas, that "God alone is the measure of all things."[2] It was probably in the autumn of 1840 that Herwegh first read Feuerbach.[3] In any case, we know that Herwegh invited Feuerbach to become a collaborator of the *Deutsche Bote* in September of 1842, and that Herwegh was sufficiently Feuerbachian in that same year to write "There is too often a conflict between love and faith, as our Feuerbach has so magnificently demonstrated in his *The Essence of Christianity*."[4]

---

* Of whom—since Hitler has clasped him to his breast—may we *not* have to apply Joseph Roy's aphorism, from the preface to Feuerbach's *La Réligion* (p. ix), "Tell me to what sort of reader you address yourself, and I will know who you are."

[1] cf. Fleury, *Le poète Herwegh*, Paris, 1911, p. 341.

[2] Herwegh, *Kritische Aufsätze—1839 und 1840*, Belle-Vue, 1845, p. 38.

[3] cf. Lévy, op. cit., p. 430.   [4] Ibid., p. 438.

We know also that it was at about this time that Herwegh lost all the vestiges of his Platonism and Hegelianism. In his pocket notebook, for example, he wrote "Hegel is a corpse upon the battlefield; Feuerbach passes over him to advance; Schelling passes over him to flee."[1]

The essentially new and important chord which Herwegh struck in his poetry was that the heights in which poets had always dwelt were empty; the earth below, he avers, is impregnated with human material from which the most lofty ideals may be drawn. He was among the first to oppose revolutionary art to romantic art, in the same manner in which Feuerbach opposed the philosophy of the future with the transcendental, supernaturalist philosophy of the past. To the artists who wish to sacrifice earthly life and earthly beauty to the supernatural spirit, he counters that earthly life and earthly beauty will carry off the victory in the coming battle between the human and the ascetic ideal. He enjoined literature to incarnate a new deity in the world, adjoining sacredness to terrestrial beauty. One among his *Poems of the Living Man* reads:

"Day to day life is the madonna of poets
   The *Mater dolorosa* who must bear
   The Saviour. Respect the epoch wherein thou livest . . .
   Naught thou canst envision is half so rare."[2]

It was at the outset Feuerbach's humanism which caught the imagination of Herwegh. The latter saw in it the kernel of a new religion which decided him to renounce his former faith. He expressly asserted that man has no longer any

---

[1] Lévy, op. cit., p. 438.   [2] Quoted by Lévy, op. cit., p. 437.

right to accept the consolations of Christian orthodoxy, for the Church can do nothing to remedy the evils of society. He esteemed that no matter what measures might be taken to bolster up Christianity, they would only serve to accelerate its fall, for the oppressed and disinherited would increasingly see that the official preservers of the faith protect religion only through self-interest. Some of his most striking verses, in this connection, are those which he wrote about the Hamburg fire and the construction of the cathedral of Cologne. "Do not build churches," he said, "for the poor do not even have huts."[1]

It was particularly during a trip to Rome that Herwegh, both in verse and in prose, expressed his feelings concerning the irreducible conflict between Christianity and humanism, and his hopes that men might cease to venerate God and commence to honour man. "That Rome 'which was but a cinder without fire, the funereal urn of the world, famous for its dead,' fortified in him the desire for a truly human life."[2] For he dreamed of a world in which men would cease to reach out for a heaven, but would be free and proud on earth. Herwegh rejected immortality; he was a Feuerbachian here too. We see it well in his sonnets XVIII and XIX, from which we take a few typical lines:

> "Long live death, friends; yes, long live death!
> In the depths of the night I have kindled a flame.
> My breath
> Spend I singing to honour the earth's most faithful.
> 'Tis the dead whom I wish to exalt—and death."

[1] Lévy, op. cit., p. 436.
[2] Lévy, op. cit., p. 439.

And again:

> "Death is not bitter. Were it not, we
> Would demand it, to give life entirety.
> The heart needs must stop in the human breast
> Ere it beat in the breast of humanity."[1]

Herwegh was much preoccupied with the problem of liberty. He inveighs—and in this he is thoroughly Feuerbachian—against the unholy alliance between liberty, even as a concept, and religion. Thus in criticizing an article by Maerker on "Hegel and Christian Liberty," he writes: "Christian liberty! It is true that Christianity preaches liberty, but the idea of liberty existed long before there was a Christianity. Liberty is liberty. It is neither Turk, nor pagan, nor Christian. Liberty has but one faith: in itself."[2] The question of liberty was, in a Feuerbachian sense, a religious question for Herwegh. And it was thus that it was a political question also. He protested against such poets as Hoffmann and Fallersleben who used the concept of liberty in an exclusively transcendental sense, calling for human liberty in the name of God rather than in the name of man. To Herwegh, furthermore, absolute monarchy and celestial tyranny were virtually identical. Thus he drew a frankly political conclusion from the substance of Feuerbachianism. And he sought to lead Feuerbach into the political activity toward which, in Herwegh's estimation, Feuerbachianism pointed. For he thought Feuerbach to be more of a revolutionist in the strict political sense than Feuerbach actually was.

[1] Quoted by Lévy, ibid., p. 433.
[2] Herwegh, op. cit., p. 79.

In a letter to Feuerbach written December 3, 1851, Herwegh said: "Come to Switzerland. Wagner very much wishes you to. Since my friend Bakunin is dead I know no one who has a more truly revolutionary character, from the point of view both of sentiments and intelligence, than yourself and Wagner."[1] It is in answer to this and similar entreaties to occupy himself more with the political consequences of his philosophy that Feuerbach replied to Herwegh: "It is the role of the Germans to study the imponderable elements of history. The French, on the other hand, are taken in by everything which is ponderable and draw the consequences before the latter are ripe. I wish, in my domain, to rest faithful to the duty of the Germans; nor do I wish to rest, since the object of my studies has not been exhausted."[2] So Herwegh pushed on, studying natural science, penning cogent verse on all sorts of political happenings, internal and external. He moved close to the position of Marx, writing his celebrated hymn to *die Partei*, and raising high the banner *"E pur si muove."** For, as he said, "It does move, and naught will stop it, neither Bavarian beer nor Prussian Christianity."[3]

But he never forgot his friend and master, who was ever happy "to breathe, in the corner in which he had ensconced himself, the perfume of Herwegh's lyrical poetry."[4] And, when Feuerbach died in 1872, the poet wrote "to his Ludwig Feuerbach" this farewell:

---

[1] *Letters to and from Georg Herwegh,* edited by Marcel Herwegh, 2nd edition, Munich, 1898, p. 12.   [2] Ibid.

* Galileo's famous under-his-breath words, "And yet it *does* move!"

[3] From Herwegh's *Poems of the Living Man,* p. 241. Quoted by Lévy, op. cit., p. 435.

[4] Lévy, op. cit., p. 442.

"Across Heaven and Hell you blazed a trail
   As the great Dante in days of yore.
Forgotten the name we called it until
   You told us: 'Human comedy—nothing more.' "[1]

*   *   *   *   *

The eminent German novelist and poet Gottfried Keller, a younger contemporary of Feuerbach, was nineteen years old the night in September 1839 when several thousand fanatical Catholic peasants, led by the pastor Hirzel, attempted a putsch against the Government which had called Strauss* to Zurich. Keller was in the fields at his uncle's farm, occupied in making hay; and, when the word spread that the peasants were marching on the city, he rushed to its defence, covering on foot the dozen or so miles which separated the farm from Zurich. He had to run along footpaths and by-roads, avoiding the main road, for if any of the peasants had caught him there they might have killed him as a *Straussien*.[2] It is evident that Keller inherited some of the Keller family radicalism, although his father died when Gottfried was but five years old. At that time the canton of Zurich was ceaselessly troubled by political agitation—the religious issue, even in the abortive *Zuri-Putsch* against Strauss, seems to have been secondary

---

[1] Herwegh, *Neue Gedichte*, Zurich, 1877, p. 266.

* The young Hegelian author of *Leben Jesu* who, proscribed by the Prussian Government, had had to take refuge in Switzerland. *Leben Jesu* had incurred for its author official wrath because of his historico-radical treatment of the Christian dogmas. He had done for Christianity in the logical domain what Feuerbach did for it in the social psychological domain.

[2] Recounted by Baldensperger, *Gottfried Keller*, Paris, Hachette.

—and Keller as a youth seems to have been not inactive in it. But when, nominally a liberal Protestant, he went away to Munich to complete his formal education he began to examine seriously the religious problem, frequenting alternately the Catholic cathedral, the Greek church, and the synagogue—all save his Protestant church. A liberal at heart, the spectacle of these coexistent religions developed in Keller a spirit of tolerance. He clearly respected traditional religious opinions; in a letter written in 1843 he says: "There is in me a tumultuous fermentation, as in a volcano. I am going to throw myself into the struggle for absolute independence and for freedom of the mind and of religious opinion."[1] In another letter he writes: "Believe me, I think of God each day, and I have confidence in Him, even though I do not make the regulation promenade every Sunday to church in order to sleep there."[2]

In his first poems Keller addresses joyous prayers to Deity. In them he dreams of a new golden age in which all men shall be of a single flock, shepherded by a simple Pastor; he ridicules atheism as bare bones. God is to him the ruling spirit in nature, the creator of all things. The stars promise us immortality. Keller is aware of the lacunae and want of perfection in much of institutional religion, but he expects it can be reformed and saved; he sees himself as a liberal agent in this reform.

Keller first knew of Feuerbach through one of the latter's lesser disciples, Marr. It seems that Keller did not take much stock in the second-hand Feuerbachianism, having relatively little respect for Marr, who "worked for nothing

[1] Baechtold, *Monographie et Correspondence de Keller*, I, p. 211.
[2] Ibid., I, p. 168.

less than the dissolution of the old world. In awaiting the final catastrophe, he lived on his father's money; he had *The Essence of Christianity* in his pocket when he strolled by the shores of the lake with black-eyed maidens, and spoke to them, undoubtedly, about the negation of faith. In his lost moments, he sought to adapt for the use of workers the platitudes of the *Religion of the Future*. Thus have Feuerbachian agitators compromised philosophy."[1]

It was not until Keller arrived at Heidelberg in his thirtieth year that he met Feuerbach. At that time he was almost immediately won over by the latter's arguments. Miss Hay tells us that "at Heidelberg he (Keller) fell in with a group of scholars, professors, and philosophers. Chief among these was Ludwig Feuerbach, the philosopher. . . . Feuerbach's philosophy, this fearless thought and wide historical knowledge, made a deep impression upon Keller . . . but he was not destined to be swept into philosophic studies, love came to his mental rescue."[2] Keller not only followed Feuerbach's lectures and read his books, but he struck up a warm personal friendship with Feuerbach, whose public star had already passed its zenith, but who was never more brilliant or persuasive. At the risk of too much quoting, we will cite excerpts from some of Keller's correspondence of that time in order better to understand the relation between the two men.

On January 29, 1849, Keller wrote to his friend Baum-

---

[1] Quoted by Lévy, op. cit., p. 501.

[2] Marie Hay, *The Story of a Swiss Poet*, Berne, 1920. The last phrase in this quotation has reference to Keller's prolonged and vain courtship of the unhappy Johanna Kapp.

gartner as follows: "The most singular thing which has here happened to me—I who, in a review of Ruge's work, attached Feuerbach in passing, the imbecile that I was; I who, not long ago, was stupid enough to quarrel with you about him—is that I find myself almost every evening in the company of this same Feuerbach; I drink beer with him, and I am suspended from his lips. . . . I find myself at the same level as Feuerbach. The world is a republic, he says, and can support neither an absolute God nor the constitutional God of the rationalists. I cannot, for the moment, resist this revolt. My God for a long time has been only a sort of president or first consul. . . . I have been forced to depose Him. . . . Immortality has been sacrificed by the same stroke. As beautiful and as rich in sentiment as this idea is, you have only to use your good sense and you find the contrary just as catching and profound. For me there were hours of solemn meditation in which I began to accustom myself to the thought of a veritable death. I can assure you that one does not lose his grasp nor become exactly worse than before. But all that, my dear Baumgartner, does not occur as easily in reality as it would seem by my letter. I defended the ground foot by foot. At the beginning, I was critical of Feuerbach's lectures. Although recognizing the acuity of his thoughts, I was establishing in a parallel series my own ideas, and I thought at first that I would only have to push differently the mechanism of these levers and stops to adapt the whole machine to my use. But after the fifth or sixth lecture, this resistance fell away little by little, and my mind finished by working on his side, for the adversary. My mute objections were conscientiously put on the carpet by the lecturer himself, who was often able to banish them more or less as I had already done in my presentiments."[1]

In another letter Keller sums up Feuerbach's effect on him in the following words: "Where are my relations with the good God? Everything is broken. Ludwig Feuerbach and the constitutionals of Frankfort, added to some summary knowledge of physiology, have debarrassed me of all luxuriant dreams. Rational monarchy is as repugnant to me in religion as in politics."[2]

Gottfried Keller had found his road to Damascus. It is not surprising, therefore, that in his second collection of poems he attacks deist immortality with as much vigour as he had previously defended it. In his first poems, the stars and the brevity of life are guarantors of immortality. In his post-1850 poems, nature and the brevity of life prove that there is no life beyond the grave. Typical lines from one of his poems of this period read:

> "In days so coldly iced with winter,
> In the shadows of hopeless Time I see
> That I must banish thee from mind,
> O vain mirage, immortality.

> "Now summer, luminous torch, is here,
> And I know well that I was right.
> I have made for my heart a better crown;
> In the tomb my illusion, black as night."[3]

In such philosophical poems as his *Sermon*, Keller shows

---

[1] Baldensperger, quoted by Lévy, op. cit., pp. 501–4.
[2] Letter to Freiligrath, April 4, 1850. Quoted by Lévy, op. cit., p. 505.
[3] Keller, *Poems*, ii, p. 18.

himself to be in accord with Feuerbach in realizing that it is most of all those who have frittered away their time on earth who demand a supplementary life in order to complete their unfinished work. In this poem Keller sketches the day of the pastor who from his pulpit preaches about immortality to his old, fatigued, and sleeping parishioners who awake at the end of the sermon to leave the church and sit lazily in the sun of the churchyard cemetery, where soon they will sleep their last sleep. The pastor, younger than most of his congregation, goes to his home where he, who in his sermon had found life too short, finds the three hours which separate him from his dinner too long. He walks in his garden where he catches a butterfly. After thus having merited immortality by his work, he goes to sleep as had his parishioners.

From the preceding it can be seen that the clergy, of which Keller was not at all intolerant in his youth, is little respected by the mature Keller. Although it is true that his Feuerbachianism made the poet intolerant of supernatural religion, he seems to have mitigated his strong feelings in this regard by a keen sense of humour. Thus we read that Keller offered a toast to a distinguished theologian at a banquet in the following speech: "Gentlemen! There are, I have remarked, two sorts of theologians: Those who consider themselves above God Almighty and those who believe they are under Him. Our friend, Herr S., has always belonged to the latter sort and so I call upon you to drink his health!"[1]

In his novel, *The Lost Smile*, Keller's two main characters, Justine and Jukundus, are shown to have lost their love

[1] Hay, op. cit., p. 125.

and their smiles because of the pressure of the world. Justine turns to religion, attending church faithfully and subscribing implicitly to the dogmas of a pastor whose religion is shown to be a sham. Jukundus is led to corruption through a political career. Both find happiness in the end through realization of the power of love of humanity and a glad acceptance of life. The lost smiles return with the realization that neither power nor money nor religion are adequate. Peace and silence, they conclude, are not death but life. Again, in *The Landvogt of Greifensee*, Solomon Landolt is shown to find meaning in life, after numerous unfortunate love affairs, in awareness of the intrinsic beauty and meaning of nature.

Philosophically, Keller was more than a Feuerbachian. In questions of religion and immortality he was, as we have seen, considerably influenced by Feuerbach. He not only paid open and covert homage to the latter in his writings, but he so tried to conform his acts to his words that he at one time ostentatiously joined a society for the cremation of the dead. He did not wish to be, he said, one of those cowards who feared being too warm when all was finished. But, as has been pointed out by devotees of Keller, he was also a Spinozist, Liebnitzian, Fichtean. This is undoubtedly true, in so far as "he sanctified the chair in which he sat, for he saw in it, in the light of Spinozism, a mode of the divine substance; when he took his coffee he noticed how his coffee pot was kept together by the pre-established harmony of monads; disciple of Fichte, he no longer believed in his nose."[1] And also, in the same quotation, "disciple of Feuerbach, he venerated himself as a God."

[1] Lévy, op. cit., p. 519.

It is true that Keller's own philosophy was eclectic. But it is also true that, in addition to being Feuerbachian in religion, Keller was also Feuerbachian in another domain, supremely important to the creative artist—in the domain of art itself. A detailed analysis of Keller's aesthetic would have to take into account the writings on aesthetics of Hettner, a disciple of Feuerbach, who was professor at Heidelberg, and had influenced Keller when he was there, as well as keeping up a correspondence with him long afterward. Not having space for this investigation, we will but quote one remark of Keller's which may serve in some measure to show how great he considered Feuerbach's influence on art in general. "For art and poetry," he wrote, "there can henceforth be no salvation without an absolute spiritual autonomy and without a burning enthusiasm for nature, without reserve and without regret; and I am absolutely convinced that no artist will henceforth be able to have a future, if he does not will to be entirely and exclusively a mortal. That is why my new evolution and the influence of Feuerbach have modified my dramatic plans and my literary hopes in a matter much more decisive than they have acted on me in other respects."[1]

In sum, Gottfried Keller's realist contribution to the philosophy of art is the same as Ludwig Feuerbach's contribution to philosophy in general. Humanity must be led back from heaven to earth.

*   *   *   *   *

We have seen that, while Herwegh—in certain respects—passed by Feuerbach and went on to a position close to that

[1] Baechtold, op. cit., ii, p. 170.

of Marx, Keller passed beyond Feuerbach only in the sense that he took the spirit of Feuerbachianism and made it into the live stuff of literature. Richard Wagner, whom we shall now consider, became a Feuerbachian and, after some time, passed on to Schopenhauer. We shall, however, here consider only the rapports between Wagner and Feuerbach. By so doing it is in no wise our intention to belittle Schopenhauer's influence on Wagner or to claim any monopoly of influence for Feuerbach. We are concerned solely with demonstrating the way in which Feuerbach's philosophy became a vital, living, positive force in certain of his contemporaries; and, collaterally, with demonstrating certain aspects of Feuerbach's philosophy which became clearer as they are mirrored by these contemporaries.

There is far from unanimity on the part of Wagnerians as to the exact influence of Feuerbach on Wagner. It is indisputable that Wagner did not at any time know Feuerbach intimately as had Herwegh and Keller, but it is equally indisputable that Wagner overtly expressed admiration for Feuerbach as early as in 1850, in dedicating his *Work of Art and the Future* to him. It is, however, the contention of such commentators as Chamberlain[1] and Lichtenberger[2] that Wagner had at this time read but one work of Feuerbach's, his first, *Thoughts on Death and Immortality*. Both these commentators draw therefrom the conclusion that Wagner could not have been much of a Feuerbachian. Leaving aside the question as to whether Wagner had or had not read *The Essence of Christianity* or others of Feuerbach's works written in the late 1830's and in the 1840's

---

[1] H. S. Chamberlain, *R. Wagner.*
[2] Lichtenberger, *R. Wagner, poète et penseur,* Paris, Alcan.

(Lévy adduces considerable evidence to prove that he had[1]), the criticisms of the two mentioned Wagnerians do not seem very important. The important fact is whether Wagner understood the essence of Feuerbachianism and whether or not he agreed with it and was influenced by it, not whether he had read one book or six. For light upon this point we must turn to Wagner's works themselves.

The first of Wagner's works in which appears what is, we submit, the clear imprint of Feuerbach is the unfinished drama, *Jesus of Nazareth*. One of the first striking phrases in this drama is "The kingdom of heaven is not outside us, but is within us. That is why those below who follow my commandments are happy and possess the kingdom of heaven."[2] This sounds inspired, at least in part, by *Thoughts on Death and Immortality*. On the same page of *Jesus of Nazareth* we read how man participates in immortality by uniting himself with immanent God through love. "Just as the body has numerous and varied members, each of which has its function, its utility, and its particular character, although together they form but a single body, just so are all men members of a single God. But God is Father and Son; He reproduces Himself ceaselessly; in the Father was the Son, and in the Son is the Father. As we are members of a single body which is God and whose breath is love eternal, we will never die, just as the body, God, never dies because he is Father and Son; that is, He is the constant realization of eternal love itself."[3]

Further on in the drama Wagner enunciates a Feuer-

---

[1] Lévy, op. cit., chap. ix.
[2] Wagner, *Jesus von Nazareth*, Leipzig, 1887, p. 39.
[3] *Jesus von Nazareth*, p. 39.

bachian theme with reference to immortality. Death, he proclaims, is absorbed by love. It is an act of sacrifice which immediately finds its recompense since it is simultaneously "moral devotion and metaphysical beatitude." In leaving this life one enters forthwith the divine life.* "The temple of God," adds Wagner, "is humanity."[1] One other note struck in the drama is markedly Feuerbachian, close, in fact, to the discussion of the Trinity in *The Essence of Christianity*. Wagner says that God is Father, Son, and Holy Spirit, "for the Father engenders the Son throughout all time, and, reciprocally, the Son engenders the Father of the Son throughout all eternity: This is life and love; this is the Holy Spirit."[2] The role of the Holy Spirit is here analogous to that enunciated by Feuerbach, with the exception that a maternal side of the Holy Spirit is not expressed.

By the foregoing can we answer the Wagnerians who state that Wagner was never basically Feuerbachian and that he had not read Feuerbach before 1850.† The passages from *Jesus of Nazareth* which we have just cited were written in 1848.

The direct reference to Feuerbach in the dedication to the *Work of Art and the Future* has been mentioned. In addition, we find in a letter from Wagner to Karl Ritter, dated November 21, 1849, the following: "Feuerbach ends by absorbing himself in man, and it is in this that he is so important, particularly in opposition to absolute philosophy,

---

* Compare this with the previously quoted lines from Herwegh's sonnets.

[1] *Jesus von Nazareth*, p. 50. [2] Ibid., p. 27.

† We discuss this point only because upon it hinges the assertions of Chamberlain and Lichtenberger that Wagner's ideas were in virtually no sense derived from Feuerbach.

which tends to absorb man in philosophy."[1] Again in the introduction to the third and fourth volumes of his collected works Wagner speaks of Feuerbach in this wise: "At that time I had read several works of Feuerbach's which interested me intensely. I borrowed from him different formulas which I applied to artistic representations, to which they could not always exactly correspond, however. In this I let myself be guided without critical reflection by an ingenious writer who appeared to be in line with the sentiments which I then had, particularly in so far as he took leave of philosophy (in which he believed to have found solely disguised theology) and inclined toward a conception of the human essence, in which I thought to recognize distinctly my ideal of man the artist."[2] Wagner further distinctly mentions the terms which he borrowed from Feuerbach, among them being "necessity," "sensibility," and "communism."

An extended discussion of the relation between Feuerbach and Wagner as manifested in the latter's *Work of Art and the Future* is outside the scope of these pages.* In it Wagner does, however, not only borrow Feuerbachian terminology, but he accepts Feuerbach's whole doctrine as a base upon which to construct his theory. He tries, in a definite way, to carry out Feuerbach's thesis. The pervading idea contained in the work can be summed up roughly as follows: There is an underlying harmony between the laws of nature on the one hand and human

[1] cf. Wagner's *Briefe*, Leipzig, Fritsch; cited by Lévy, op. cit., p. 458.

[2] cf. Wagner, *Werke*, Leipzig, Fritsch; Introduction to vols. iii and iv.

* Such a discussion will be found in the ninth chapter of Lévy's work on Feuerbach as well as, from a different point of view, in the works of Houston Stewart Chamberlain and Lichtenberger on Wagner.

conduct on the other. The former express the real conditions of life; the latter, the artistic ideal. This harmony has been concealed and disturbed by what both Feuerbach and Wagner called the *Willkür*, the arbitrary (as distinguished from the necessary). The arbitrary are religions, abstract metaphysics, and egoistic, artificial social institutions. The work of art of the future will only be possible if this disharmony is destroyed and the underlying natural harmony restored. The source of this restoration will be communism —loosely defined—to be created out of the sheer necessity of the people. The restoration's ideal will derive from the essence of humanity; its means will be the union of all the arts heretofore separated; and its interpreters will be the newly associated artists. In sketching this system, Wagner defines the mediating link between humanity and nature as love; not revealed love from on high, but ordinary human love. This, he asserts, is the most active manifestation of human life, the principle of all true art and beauty, which latter previously had been but an abstract ideal drawn not from real life but from Greek aesthetics. The work of art of the future, says Wagner elsewhere, will be "the dramatic representation of the myth* justified by the clearest human conscience and brought back to the view of present life."[1]

Without analysing this position in any greater detail, we may observe that Wagner's disharmony between natural necessity and human morality is but a variation of Feuerbach's theme on the contradiction between faith and love;

---

* Wagner defines the myth as the symbolically expressed conception of the harmonious common life of the past.

[1] Wagner, *Oper und Drama*, p. 88.

and that Feuerbachian and Wagnerian love are practically identical concepts. Further, the poet represents the beautiful exactly as the philosopher had defined the good and the true. In one respect worth mentioning, however, Wagner draws consequences beyond Feuerbachianism just as we have seen in Herwegh. In his *Opera and Drama*, Wagner analyses religion* further, and from his central thought— the rehabilitation of the spirit of the myth—he concludes that religion ought to reabsorb the state which is its alienation. Political revolution appears to Wagner the necessary precondition of the artistic revolution. The state, an arbitrary construction which has been substituted for the primitive community, must be abolished; and likewise the whole system of law, an arbitrary contract which has been substituted for natural custom. The meta-Feuerbachian, half-Marxian, overtones of this conclusion are patent.

From this point Wagner outlines the changes which would take place in the domain of art after the wiping out of the political state. The artist would address himself to sentiment rather than thought; the arbitrary state makes for "abstract individuality," expressible only by thought. He would, from his youth, acquire uniform artistic habits, surmounting the arbitrary barriers which prevent the presentation of a faithful image of life. Age would no longer oppose itself, in the name of vain experience, to the drives which push youth to action; it would, on the contrary, and thanks to love and serenity, better justify the acts of youth than youth itself; it would know how to explain them and

* Religion is of equal import, according to Wagner, for the artist as for the philosopher or theologian. Because the work of art is only the translation or communication of the religious ideal.

give a conscientious representation of them.[1] "Wagner considers that the myth is at the beginning and the end of history, just as sentiment is both anterior and posterior to reason; lyricism is at the origin and terminus of poetry; music is the principle and the full flower of spoken language. It may be said that this tendency to conciliate in a higher synthesis the faculties which have successively dominated humanity was one of the profoundest traits of Wagner's personal character. It can be maintained, to be sure, that the whole nineteenth century moved in this direction. It would seem, nevertheless, permissible to affirm that Feuerbach gave Wagner a clearer conscience of the direction to follow and furnished him with more than one point of repair."[2]

Wagner was aware of certain oscillations of emphasis in his own work. He makes mention of this in his *Communication to my Friends,* where he insists on the necessity of taking into account the "monumental critic," Time, in order to explain his artistic evolution.[3] This difference of emphasis is evident by comparison of, among his earlier works, *Tannhäuser* and *Lohengrin.* In the former Wagner seems to want to leave the frivolous and sensual world, to ascend toward the heights, to find purity, fresh air, and objectivity in looking down upon the petty world below. In the latter, again, Wagner turns back again to the earth to grope in the world of imperfect men for his ideal. In

[1] cf. Wagner's *Werke,* vol. iv, p. 72.   [2] Lévy, op. cit., pp. 482–3.
[3] Wagner, *Werke,* vol. iv, p. 244. His discussion of time here is, incidentally, close to that of Feuerbach in the introduction to *Thoughts on Death and Immortality.* Time is an essential category of the musical understanding. It would be painful, he points out, for a man with a sense of music to hear executed a mixture of Bach and Beethoven.

comparing both of these to the *Nibelungen Ring*, we see how the composer's Feuerbachianism helps synthesize these two opposing tendencies. Siegfried is the personification of love in nature, the man-god who reunites heaven and earth. He is a symbol of the restitution of its essence to humanity. The twilight of the gods is the dawn of the humanity of the future over which neither gold nor power will reign, but only love. Wotan is the father who expresses the conflict between the arbitrary and the natural. Tied to the world by the former, he nevertheless hopes for his children the joy, love, and freedom represented by the latter. He dies to make this possible. The role of Brunnhilde does not, as Schopenhauerians insist, express a negation of the will to live. Her annunciation of the reign of love and her heroic devotion to humanity, shown by her voluntary death, are much more Feuerbachian.

In what respects, then, is Wagner Schopenhauerian? Herwegh, we are told, brought Wagner a copy of *The World as Will and Representation* in 1854.[1] It was after this that traces of pessimism began to creep into his works. Thus he wrote to Liszt "Do not consider the world except to mistrust it!"[2] This pessimism deepened as Wagner grew older; the lamentable failure of the Revolution in 1848 grew bitterer and bitterer in the memory of the poet who had started out with rather messianic illusions. And thus, toward the middle of his life, he pretended to abandon his old testament prophet, Feuerbach, for a new testament prophet,

[1] cf. Lévy, op. cit., p. 449. In disproof of the allegations of Schopenhauerianism in the *Nibelungen Ring* it is only necessary to point out that Wagner, according to H. S. Chamberlain, sketched the outlines of the whole *Ring* in 1852, two years before he had read Schopenhauer.

[2] Lichtenberger op. cit., p. 309.

Schopenhauer. But he never ceased to work for the humanity of the future, and even though destiny intervened to separate them and make them cease to understand one another, yet Feuerbach and Wagner, "even when they thought themselves adversaries—these two Germans of the nineteenth century, protestants and humanists, workers for reform and renaissance—they were still brothers."[1]

We cannot, unfortunately, close this chapter without reference to another side of Wagner, neither Feuerbachian nor Schopenhauerian. It was the side represented by his campaign against "Judaism in music," and his other campaign under the protecting (?) wing of the Catholic king of Bavaria for a regeneration of the "true Germanic Christianity." Whence these ideas came, it is not the purpose of this book to analyse. One of them was expressed in Hegel; the other has a longer and even more grievous history. It is extremely doubtful, however, whether either Hegel or Wagner could countenance in the slightest measure the diabolical uses to which these ideas have been put. Yet they will doubtless have to share, with too many others, the indictment of history.

[1] Lévy, op. cit., p. 492.

Chapter V

PHILOSOPHY OF THE FUTURE

We have seen enough of Feuerbach, both in his own work and as reflected through that of his literary contemporaries mentioned in the last chapter, to strike a preliminary balance, to put the regrettable but necessary labels on the various aspects of his philosophy. Although Feuerbach was not a system-maker like Kant or Hegel, it is only in attempting to assess him somewhat systematically that we can see him in perspective. If this latter is not a sufficient end in itself—which we maintain that it is—it is certainly justifiable as means to the end contained in the next chapter. Feuerbach, for good or ill, is the bridge between Hegel and Marx in the history of philosophy. To a certain extent the preceding chapters are but the piled-up major girders for that bridge; we must now fit them together. A small amount of additional material will be necessary for the completion of the structure.

In the following we shall broadly consider Feuerbach's humanism,* his sensationalism, his ethics, and his metaphysics. These few categories are not, of course, either exhaustive† or mutually exclusive, but they will, in very general terms, suffice for our present purpose.

* This term we use in the very general sense in which it is often used by historians of philosophy. It is not to be confused with any specific humanist philosophy of today.

† We purposely omit here the philosophy of religion, extensively treated in Chapter II.

Before proceeding to the *seriatim* consideration of these four categories, we must say a general word about Feuerbach as the philosopher, one of whose most-repeated dicta is his "My philosophy is no philosophy." The dictum is true in the sense that Feuerbach rejected traditional philosophy, just as he rejected traditional religion. But the fact that he wished to found no new school or church in the institutional sense does not mean that he did not wish his outlook and insights to be widespread. His writings he characterized as manifestoes to humanity; he did not avoid using the term "philosophy" with reference to himself;* he referred to himself, rather, as the philosopher of the common man. Just as, in fact, he sought to substitute a new religion for the old, so he sought to develop a new philosophy. It was, for better or for worse, the first major enunciation of the new philosophy of science. For, before him, speculative philosophy had largely considered itself above empirical science, and empirical science itself had been inarticulate in any save the most specific matters.† This was because speculation and science considered themselves to be of different orders. As Feuerbach phrased it, "In speculative philosophy I miss the element of empiricism and in empiricism the elements of speculation. My method therefore is to unite both, not as two different materials, but as different prin-

---

* cf. his letter to Bolin in which he declares "They still do not see that I have no other philosophy than an inescapable one. . . ." Cited by Grün, op. cit., vol. ii, p. 191.

† This does not, of course, refer to times long gone by when science was but a subdivision of philosophy, but rather to the situation extant at the time of the rise of modern science, the latter being specifically characterized in contrast to earlier science by its controlled experimentation.

ciples, i.e. empirical *activity* and speculative *activity*."[1] Feuerbach's philosophy thus was not "no philosophy"* but, rather, a new kind of philosophy, concerned with the findings and principles of natural science, and—to a lesser extent—with the mediation between these and principles previously enunciated and developed by speculative metaphysics. We shall return to this latter point in discussing Feuerbach's sensationalism.

To go back to our four previously enunciated categories, the first of which is humanism. We have already discussed at some length the anthropocentricity of Feuerbach's philosophy of religion; he leaves us in no doubt concerning it. We shall, however, recapitulate it in quoting from the introductory remarks to the first edition of his collected works. This passage is of extra interest as an advance refutation of certain criticisms of which we shall take cognizance in the next chapter. For it was written in 1846, one year before the *Communist Manifesto* and two years before the abortive Revolution of 1848. "It will perhaps be asserted," he said, "that my present position is already passed and obsolete; the new generation wants social and political reform; it cares little for things religious, less for things philosophic. Religion is for these young men an indifferent question, or at least one that has been a long time resolved. The question is no longer one of the existence or non-existence of God, but of the existence or non-existence of men; it is no longer a question of knowing whether God is of the same or of a different essence than men, but rather

---

[1] Feuerbach, *Sämmtliche Werke*, vol. ii, p. 176.

* Unless one very narrowly define philosophy as being concerned uniquely with matters supernatural.

of knowing whether there is equality or inequality between we men; it is no longer a question or knowing how man will find justice before God, but how he will find justice before other men; it is no longer a question of knowing if and how we taste in the bread the body of the Lord, it is a question of having bread for our own bodies; it is not a question of rendering unto God what belongs to God and to the emperor what belongs to the emperor; it is a question of finally giving to man what belongs to man; it is no longer a question of being Christians or pagans, deists or atheists, but it is a question of being or becoming men, men healthy of body and soul, free, having the vitality to act and to live. I accord you all that, gentleman; that is precisely what I want, too. The question of knowing whether there is a God or not, the opposition between deism and atheism, belongs to the seventeenth and eighteenth centuries, not to the nineteenth. 'I deny God' means to me 'I deny the negation of man'; to the fantastic, illusory, and celestial position of man, which has as a necessary consequence in real life the negation of man, I substitute the sensible and real position whose necessary consequence is the social and political position of man. The question of the existence or non-existence of God is to me precisely the question of the non-existence or existence of man. Doubtless I will only cure ills which have their origin in the head or the heart; and it is from the stomach that men principally suffer. 'I feel,' said a criminal, 'as though evil thoughts were mounting from my stomach.' That criminal is the image of human society to-day. Some have all that their avid tastes could desire; others have not even that which is strictly necessary for their stomachs. Thence, you say, come all ills and all suffering, even the diseases of the head and heart of man. Consequently everything that does not tend to define or extirpate this fundamental evil is but useless rubbish. But it is of this rubbish that my complete works are made up. Alas! Yes. But are there not, none the less, many ills, even ills of the stomach, which come from the head? For my part I propose once and for all, under the influence of psychological tendencies and external circumstances, to determine and to cure the maladies of the head and of the heart of humanity."[1]

The preceding quotation shows us two things: First, that Feuerbach is interested in man, and secondly, in what parts or aspects of man he is interested. It thereby marks not only Feuerbach's separation from his philosophical past but also his separation from his politico-philosophical future. But we are anticipating ourselves.

Feuerbach's analysis of the rise of various systems of philosophy is, in general terms, Hegelian.* Each new philosophy, he points out, arises to satisfy either an intellectual or a human need. The former occurs *within* a given historical epoch; the latter marks the end of one and the beginning of another. The downfall of Christianity, caused to a considerable degree by the fruits of the Hegelian system, represents the end of one such epoch and the beginning of

---

[1] *Sämmtliche Werke*, vol. i, Introduction; quoted by Lévy, op. cit., pp. 47–9. A part of this is also cited by Hook, op. cit., pp. 222–3. In failing to quote the last ten sentences here quoted, however, Hook makes Feuerbach—on the basis of this quotation—appear to be closer to Marx than he really is.

* The general outline which follows is taken from Feuerbach's *Vorläufigen Thesen zur Reform der Philosophie*, and his principal work on the philosophy of the future, *Grundsätze der Philosophie der Zukunft*. The former was first published in 1842, the latter in 1843.

another. Feuerbach sees himself as representative of the opening era. Having analysed the needs of the latter with a view to determining what would be its philosophical expression, he concludes that the most essential drive of man has become one for social and political freedom. Thus the new philosophy must be one to suit the situation; it must proclaim new principles based on the true nature of man. Its task will be to clear the decks for action by sweeping away the remnants of speculative supernaturalism and to unify the various efforts, empirical and critical philosophical, which are inchoately preparing the general programme for human emancipation from the bondage of philosophical dualism and social undemocracy. All this Feuerbach envisages and expresses in religious terminology. The state is the religion of politics; the political representatives of the new era must substitute doubt for faith, reason for the Bible, earth for heaven, material want for hell, work for prayer, and the state of Prussia for the City of God. The new philosophy, in short, must be of and for man.

Although Feuerbach insists that he has broken with all previous philosophical constructions, he writes here very much like a nineteenth-century Protagoras. "Whatever the world is, it at least is what it looks like to man and his body. It is no less real nor more real than what it appears to those creatures who see with different eyes, touch with different 'hands,' hear with different ears—save that the whole comparison is fantastic, for we can never know how things appear to other organisms."[1] Nature is never conceived in isolation, or even set apart from man for examina-

[1] cf. Hook, op. cit., p. 258.

150

tion. Taking advantage of what has in twentieth-century epistemology been called "the egocentric predicament,"* Feuerbach decries the years of vain speculation which have been wasted on the distinction between things in themselves and things as they appear to us. Such a distinction would only be meaningful if we could see things as they do not appear to us. But this is absurd. No matter in what flights of imagination we try to envision things, symbolically, upside-down, or metaphorically, *we* see them. "When I speak of how things might appear to God, I am simply writing Him large and askew in letters of my own nature."[1] We have seen in detail how this works out in religion in Chapter II. But man is not only the secret of religion, he is the secret of politics,† history, and nature.[2] There is but one meaningful distinction between appearance and reality and this, far from driving us toward speculative transcendentalism, drives us back to man more definitely than ever. This distinction is to be found on the social plane, in the contrast between the way in which a given object may appear to a specified individual and the way in which it appears to other individuals. Feuerbach had expressed it thusly in *The Essence of Christianity*, "That is true in which another agrees with me—agreement is the first criterion of truth . . . the species is the ultimate measure of truth."[3]

The otherwise metaphysical problem of truth, then, is

* The expression is Professor Ralph Barton Perry's.

[1] Ibid., p. 257.

† This may seem like a commonplace today, but it was much less so a century ago, when politics were officially Hegelian, i.e. when there was a close kinship between the two absolutes—Idea and monarchy.

[2] cf. Feuerbach, *Sämmtliche Werke*, vol. ii, p. 264.

[3] Feuerbach, *The Essence of Christianity*, p. 158.

also approached in a humanist fashion. Rejecting the logical consistence theory and the metaphysical correspondence theory of truth, Feuerbach proclaims a theory which is closely akin to the modern pragmatist theory, save for omission of the explicit emphasis on human practice as criterion. To Feuerbach not only are sensible perceptions what they appear to be to the individual's sense organs, but truths are truths as they appear to our minds. There are, in this view, no inherent truths of reason, as the logicians aver. "It is man who thinks . . . not Reason . . . when the old philosophy therefore says only the reasonable is the true and real,* the new philosophy responds, 'only the human is the true and real,' for only what is human can be reasonable. Man is the measure of reason."[1] True, there is, as the idealists have always insisted, a principle of reason which transcends the individual human being. But this is not a transcendent principle. It is, rather, a principle which pervades the human species. The species acts as a check upon the individual. The measure of truth is humanity, the sum of the traditional, communicated, critical experience of humanity. Truth, then, is not eternal, save in the sense that humanity is eternal. Truth is progressively revealed by humanity, not by individuals. Individual experience *per se* is neutral; the tag of truth or falsity can be applied only after a given experience has been certified by the experience of more individuals.

Thus are retained the distinction between subjective and objective, and place for the necessary possibility of egoistic error, without recourse to immutable, eternal, transcendent

* Specific reference to Hegel is patently here intended.
[1] Feuerbach, *Sämmtliche Werke*, vol. ii, p. 339.

standards of truth, although some of the inescapable particular dangers of relativism are retained also.*

*   *   *   *   *

We proceed now to consideration of the second of our
general categories, sensationalism.

It can be said that to Feuerbach sensory experience was
the unique way of "getting at" existence. In the widest
sense, both his psychology, his methodology, and his
epistemology were sensationalist. Commentators have remarked that, instead of Descartes' "Cogito, ergo sum,"
Feuerbach proclaimed a "Sentio, ergo sum." To him a
reason which did not depart from, frequently consult, and
return to sense-experience was in no sense reasonable. In

* For in this theory there is obviously considerable "lag" in the
unfolding of specific truth. (We are not now considering what might be
called primary, general truths, i.e. that man thinks, feels, eats, kills, does
good, etc.) Thus before the time of Christopher Columbus, humanity—or
the representative section of humanity available at the moment—could
certify that any given individual's conception of the world as flat was
correct, was a truth. Subsequent individual experience (Columbus's),
certified by another section of humanity (his crew and the three or four
100-per-cent Americans he brought back) represented a new unfolding of
truth. And this latter truth proved that the previously accepted truth,
i.e. that the world was flat, was, in fact, *never* a truth. This, it is answered,
only proves that we have to take into account time. Agreed, but it also
means that no one can ever irrefutably assert specific truth. For there is
always the possibility that humanity will, in time, countermand that
verdict. Perhaps, to illustrate, the world is not a sphere slightly squashed
at the poles; it may be an inverted trapezoid whose "true" dimensions
will only be clear to the dry eye of the future. We raise this point because
it is one of the crucial points for a humanist theory of truth. Granted, the
latter does not pretend to be eternal, but it is difficult to see how, in any profound sense, it is ever operable with respect to specific truths. We are left to
the conclusion that the traditional definition of truth is no longer meaningful, that truth is always changing and unfolding, dialectical, if you will.

153

defining the task of philosophy, he remarks, "The task of philosophy, of science in general, consists not in getting away from the sensible, real things, but in going towards them, not in transforming objects into thoughts and representations, but in making what was invisible to common eyes visible, i.e. in making it objective."[1] Philosophy, then, has not as its task the taking of sense data and abstractly giving them meaning, but of putting sense data in such a relation that they will tell their own story. This they can do because only sensible things are real things. "Truth, Reality, sensibility are identical. Only a sensible being is a true, a real being; only sensibility is truth and reality."[2]

How is the content, the essence of things, communicated? By the senses, direct, is Feuerbach's first answer. "We feel not only stones and wood, not only flesh and bone, we feel also feelings when we press the hands or lips of a feeling creature; we catch by the ears not only the rushing of the water and the rustling of the leaves, but also the earnest voice of love and wisdom; we see not only mirror surfaces and coloured figures, but we look into the glance of man. Not the external, then, but also the internal, not only flesh but spirit, not only the thing but the Ego is an object of the senses. Everything, therefore, is sensibly apprehensible; if not immediately, at least mediately; if not with the vulgar, untrained senses, at least with the cultivated senses; if not

[1] Feuerbach, *Sämmtliche Werke*, vol. ii, p. 331. We have previously noted Feuerbach's emphasis on visual sensation. Indeed, a whole book could be written on this subject alone. For an interesting general treatment of the relation of sight to reason, see Grandjean, *La Raison et la Vue*, Geneva, 1919.

[2] Feuerbach, *Grundsätze der Philosophie der Zukunft*, Leipzig, 1849, Section 32.

with the eye of the anatomist or chemist, at least with the eye of the philosopher."[1]

It is only the "if not immediately, at least mediately" which saves the foregoing from being a ridiculously over-simplified overstatement. Its motivation was Feuerbach's desire to combat abstract rationalism, which, he avers, had completely deserted sense experience. But obviously the question as to the manner in which raw sense experience arranges itself to be made material for the understanding poses itself. To answer it Feuerbach had to back up a bit from the position established in this quotation and admit that certain discriminatory characters are given to our senses and that it is with these that we arrange the undifferentiated stuff of sensation. " 'With our senses,' I once wrote, 'we read the book of nature, but we do not understand it through them! Correct! But the book of nature is not composed of a chaos of letters strewn helter-skelter so that the under-standing must first introduce order and connection into the chaos. The relations in which they are expressed in a meaningful proposition then become the subjective and arbitrary creations of the understanding. No, we distin-guish and unify things through our understanding on the basis of certain characters of unity and difference given to our senses. We separate what Nature has separated; we tie together what she has related; we classify natural pheno-mena in categories of ground and consequence, cause and effect, because factually, sensibly, objectively things really stand in such a relation to each other."[2] Feuerbach does,

---

[1] Ibid., Sections 40–42.

[2] Feuerbach, *Sämmtliche Werke*, vol. ii, pp. 322–3; quoted by Hook, op. cit., pp. 266–7.

then, in effect admit a certain mental principle prior to sense experience. It is not completely clear whence this principle comes. At times—as in the latter quotation—it is a datum; at other times it seems to be a product of previous sensory experience. In any case, despite Feuerbach's particular emphasis on sensibility, individual sense experience is not throughout his philosophy a unique determinant of reality, for, as we have already seen in his approach to truth, the testimony of the senses is subject to certain corroboration. In this latter respect he does, in general, maintain that sense experience has value not at the beginning, but only at the end, of intellectual inquiry. For the control of individually conceived truth is socially conceived truth. The latter is a product of the common sensations of men. But the common sensations, those upon the verity and universality of which we all come to agree, are only the result of piled-up individual sensations, of sensations in the aggregate. It is through these—experientially, by and large—that the characters of unity and difference are given to our senses.

Upon occasion—as we have already noted—Feuerbach asserts that direct sensation is ineluctable, immediate truth. At other times he asserts that direct sensation is not always true and real because of man's imagination and expectations, which so warp or condition his sensations that he gets unclear representations.* It is the task of philosophy to demonstrate the way in which the latter occurs, to guard man against immediately accepting his sense impressions. Thus the philosophy of the future is not simply a direct apology for empirical man; it sets the elevation from un-critical sense experience to critical, self-conscious sense ex-

* "Vorstellungen."

perience as its task. From this point of view Feuerbach's entire preoccupation with the philosophy of religion was only by way of clarifying man's perceptions, both of himself and of the external world of sense experience. To this latter clings another important epistemological point.

Feuerbach insists that philosophy's *point de départ* must not be philosophy itself, but the life of man. Neither, he continues, the external world nor man's mind are the *primary* facts in man's life. The primary fact is the human community, for only it, by our previous definitions, makes possible truth or meaning or even individual self-consciousness. Thus the epistemological problem of the reality or non-reality of the external world is not recognized by Feuerbach, for it is resolved by him at the very outset. The question as to whether his ideas correspond to the world which causes them, or whether there is a real world which exists independently of our consciousness is not a real question to an individual Feuerbachian. "The *social facts* of his own experience and not his psychological sense data provide the answers to the question in so far as it is a question. The very sense perception which the individual sets out to check against the external world must first be established to have veridical character by comparison with the perceptions of *others*, of the species."[1] Therefore, "as certain as the other person is a creature existing independently of me, so is the tree, the stone, an entity independent of me."[2]

To Feuerbach, as to the pragmatists, knowledge is not

---

[1] Hook, op. cit., pp. 258–9.
[2] Feuerbach, *Sämmtliche Werke*, vol. v, p. 207; quoted by Hook, op. cit., p. 259.

prior—either in the temporal or importance sense—to experience; it is the fruit of experience. Nor, once given, is knowledge divisible into subject and object constituents. The subjective and objective are differentiations which occur in the course of human activity. In social living the activity of the human subject is dependent upon the activity of the objects of the subject, be they human or inanimate. But each of these objects, speaking now in the human sense, is also a subject in its own right, and our initial human subject is object to this latter. "Subjects and objects do not come together to create human activity; they are ever changing distinctions within it."[1]

Another aspect of Feuerbach's sensationalism must be mentioned; it is what is often and properly called his "degenerate" sensationalism. We have already seen that Feuerbach identifies reality with sensibility in his *Bases of the Philosophy of the Future*.* On another occasion, after reading a now forgotten and never important scientific work,† Feuerbach pretends to find a new philosophic unity, to resolve for all time the dualisms that have been stumbling-blocks for lucid thinking, in the "revolutionary" principles of food chemistry. Philosophers had, it appeared, overlooked what was, literally, right in front of them—at meal times. Let us hear about it in Feuerbach's own words: "Sustenance only is substance. Sustenance is the identity of spirit and nature. Where there is no fat, there is no flesh, no brain, no spirit. But fat comes only from Sustenance

[1] Ibid., p. 259.

* In a few extravagant passages he even equates sensibility with love, and then says, e.g., "Love is the true ontological proof of the existence of things outside of our heads."—*Sämmtliche Werke*, vol. ii, p. 324.

† Moleschott's *Lehre der Nahrungsmittel*.

. . . the essence of essence. Everything depends upon what we eat and drink. Difference in essence is but difference in food."[1] He goes on, and, in an even more extreme manner, proceeds to fashion a gastronomocentric universe, the slogan of which is "Foodstuff is Thoughtstuff."* He even becomes explicit about the diet of certain European countries, postulating a scale of revolutionary-energy values in different foods. Thus he commiserates the potato-eating Irish in their struggle for national independence as follows: "Poor Ireland! You cannot conquer in the struggle with your stiff-necked neighbour whose luxuriant flocks supply its hirelings with strength. You cannot conquer, for your sustenance can only arouse a paralysing despair, not a fiery enthusiasm. And only enthusiasm will be able to fight off the giant in whose veins flows the rich, powerful, deed-producing, roast-beef blood."[2]

This same principle is applied to the Italians, the Hindus, and, in general, everybody whose social position might be improved. Especially does he draw the lessons of the German political disaster of 1848. The revolutionists could not emancipate themselves from political reaction because they could not rise above their penchant for potatoes. Potato blood cannot make revolutions; what future have revolutionists? Moleschott and his test tubes, it appears, have a way out. Hear the heartening words: "Shall we therefore despair? Is there no other foodstuff which can replace potatoes among the poorer classes and at the same time

---

[1] Feuerbach, *Sämmtliche Werke*, 2nd ed., vol. ii, p. 82; quoted by Hook, op. cit., p. 268.

* "Der Nahrungstoff ist Gedankenstoff."

[2] Quoted by Hook, op. cit., p. 270.

nurture them to manly vigour and disposition? Yes, there is such a foodstuff . . . which is the pledge of a better future, which contains the seeds of a more thorough even if more gradual revolution. It is —— beans!"[1]

What a revolutionary rallying cry: Beans, not potatoes!

One other phrase belongs in this section. Habitually sundered from its context, it is the blank cartridge that was heard around the world, the last sentence in the following: "We see the important ethical significance for the people of the doctrine of food. What is eaten becomes blood; blood becomes heart and brain, the material of thought and disposition. Human sustenance is the foundation of human culture and disposition. Do you want to improve the people? Then instead of preaching against sin, give them better food. Man is what he eats."[2]

Only in one sense can the patent ridiculousness of this whole doctrine be somewhat overlooked. If man is what he eats, then the main problem on humanity's agenda is not religious, metaphysical, ontological, or cultural, but economic. In the sense that deficient individual or national nutrition is to a very considerable extent responsible for crime and wars, and thus mediately at the core of many a philosophical problem, Feuerbach is completely right. On the other hand, the central problem for many people in this day and age is not how to get beans instead of potatoes in their diet, but how to get any diet at all.

Fortunately, this whole diversion is not generic to

---

[1] Hook, op. cit., p. 271.

[2] Feuerbach, *Sämmtliche Werke*, 2nd ed., vol. ii, p. 90. The euphony of the latter sentence when quoted in German ("Der Mensch ist was er isst") is one reason for its being so widespread.

Feuerbach's system, such as it is; and it therefore does not, we submit, detract from the value of Feuerbach's other insights any more than do the sun's spots prevent it from lighting and warming this our earth.

    *   *   *   *   *

We now turn to an estimation of Feuerbach's ethic of love, "tuism," as it has sometimes been called by historians of philosophy.*

At the outset we may be permitted to observe that there are, in fact, two Feuerbachian ethics. In Feuerbach's first writings he tends to maintain the Kantian, Fichtean independence of ethics as against religion and theology. He judged beliefs, and even abstract ideas, according to their moral value, finding true that which was disinterested, and finding false that which was thoroughly egoistic. He first rejected the proofs for personal immortality and the existence of God, for example, because to him they appeared to be inspired by the principle of "sufficient ambition" and therefore fundamentally egoistic.[1] In fact, all through his early, critical period—as distinct from the later period in which he was engaged in laying the groundwork for the philosophy of the future—it might be said that, in an inverse Kantian sense, he considered the negation of dogmas as a postulate of the practical reason. We shall not, however, here dwell upon this aspect of Feuerbach's ethics, but shall rather proceed to a consideration of the distinctive ethic set forth in his major and later works. This latter is an immanent ethic, the origin and point of repair of which is the human heart and nature.

* cf. Lange, op. cit., vol. ii, p. 254.   [1] cf. Lévy, op. cit., p. 156.

We have noted the way in which love resolves the enigma of immortality for Feuerbach. Antecedent to this resolution, it was love which made Feuerbach tend to reject any sort of supernatural, non-terrestrial sanction. In his earliest youth he appears to have been strongly influenced by the Christian ethic.* But in his more mature work we find the drive of human love so powerful as to insurge even against the Christian ethic. Finding fallibility to be one of the most fundamental characteristics of man, he tends to make both faults and virtues neutral. For he finds faults to be but excess virtues. His preliminary conclusion he states as follows: "The tree of life is, if not in the Bible at least in reality, the tree of the knowledge of good and evil; sin is inseparable from life. Faults are a reaction of nature against the rigid rule of morality. There are natures for which only sin is the redeemer and liberator. I tell you in truth: the greatest fault in life is never to have failed, never sinned."[1]

Having thus burned his Christian bridges behind him, Feuerbach strikes out in search of a new ethic. He searches in the nature of man; first, the individual man. But he finds that "The individual man by himself does not contain the nature of man in himself, either in himself as a moral or as a thinking being. The nature of man is contained only in the community, in the unity of man with man—a unity, however, which rests only upon the reality of the distinction of I and Thou."[2] The essential nature of man as found in the community is love. It is the unity of thought and being,

* In his student notebooks we find numerous fragments eulogizing the Christian ethic. cf. Lévy, op. cit., p. 157.

[1] From Feuerbach's *Curriculum vitae*, 1834–36; quoted by Lévy, op. cit., p. 160.

[2] Feuerbach, *Grundsätze der Philosophie der Zukunft*, Section 61.

of the I and Thou, the principle of our conduct. It satisfies the soul, explains our life, gives us both the end and goal of existence. "It is necessary to find in love that which the Christian found in faith, or to say it better, it is necessary to keep Christian love, which is Christianity's soul, and reject faith which is without love."[1] Love, then, must be the basis of the new ethic. Not Christian love, however, for Christians who love God have no love left for men. The Bible says: "He who loves not his brother whom he sees, how can he love God whom he does not see?" And Feuerbach says: "He who loves his brother whom he sees, how can he love God whom he does not see?" Here, then, is the third testament, the proclamation of the new era of humanity supplanting the Middle Ages of Christianity:

"Thou must believe, yes, believe; but believe that there is also between men a true love; that the human heart is also capable of infinite love, of the love which forgives all; that human love may also have the qualities of divine love. It is worth more to love the vainest and most unworthy object than to enclose oneself without love in oneself. Love and thou wilt have all other virtues in superabundance, for there is only one Evil: Egoism, and only one Good: Love."[2]

Feuerbach was not, however, able to hold to this unqualified love for long. True, it seems to have been his guiding principle in *The Essence of Christianity*, but this is partly because, in order to analyse Christianity, he took the Christians at their, rather than his, word. Furthermore, the transition from God-orientation to man-orientation was

---

[1] Lévy, op. cit., p. 160.
[2] Feuerbach, *Curriculum vitae*, 1834–36, quoted by Lévy, op. cit., p. 161.

most swiftly and thoroughly effected by the use of this immanent principle in an unqualified manner. But once having effected the transition from heaven to earth, i.e. by the time he was faced with the task of constructing the philosophy of the future, Feuerbach found out that the category of love did not subsume all he found in man. To love he had to adjoin reason or intelligence, for love without reason is indistinguishable in its acts and in its consequences from malice or hatred. He thus arrived at this supplementary formula: "The I is reason; the Thou is love. Love with reason or reason with love is spirit."[1] His concept of love became limited externally by reason, and internally by egoism. For at the same time it became evident to him that the love of self and the love of another stem from the same source, that egoism was therefore necessary if only as an interior demarcation between self and others. Furthermore, the simple fact that parenthood is, in a definite sense, an assertion of the ego necessitated a less intransigeant stand *vis-à-vis* egoism.

But let us consider, first, the more general orientation of morality. From the beginning Feuerbach's ethic took on a different character from most other ethics. From the moment that he made man the measure of all things, Feuerbach could no longer admit an absolute. He did not, then, as he is sometimes accused of doing, make a religious principle of his ethic. The unmitigated egoist (philosophically speaking), Stirner, had asserted that the Feuerbachian morality was religious. To him Feuerbach replied: "Doubtless, in taking Christianity as point of departure, and in defining humanism by opposition to this Christianity,

[1] cf. Lévy, op. cit., p. 162.

one is led to say that ethics is the true religion; it is thereby affirmed that it is not necessary to make the rapports between men depend upon their rapports with God; an ethics which passes beyond the authority of faith is admitted; but it is not pretended that man is made for ethics. Ethics, in fact, are made for man."[1]

Apply this, then, to the hypothetical situation always raised by believers in a transcendent ethic to disprove a non-transcendent ethic. If this earth is all, who would voluntarily leave it? Who would negate himself except at the command of an absolute, transcendent ethic? The early Christians sacrificed themselves almost prodigally, for the promise of a luxurious future life was so real to them that they were not conscious of giving up anything. But today, too, people sacrifice their lives when they judge such acts of devotion necessary, even though they may not be believers in immortality; thus their *sacrifice* is more real. It is just because morality is immanent that supreme self-sacrifice is "natural" (the very word tells us the secret) for certain people. Take, on the one hand, the glorious and triumphant end of such exclusive humanists of our time as Sacco and Vanzetti.* On the other hand, "The time is passed when faithful Christians expose themselves to martyrdom; in our time it is in speaking of eternal salvation that one acquires earthly goods. . . . The true friends of Christ are now the rebels; the official protectors of the faith no longer think of

[1] cf. Lévy, op. cit., p. 163.

* cf. Vanzetti's speech after his condemnation to death, "If it had not been for these things, I might have lived out my life talking at street corners to scorning men. I might have died, unmarked, unknown, a failure. Now we are not a failure. This is our career and triumph."—Quoted by Lamont, op. cit., p. 239.

risking their lives to suppress terrestrial injustice. The dogma of the beyond no longer inspires heroic devotion; it entertains, on the other hand, the resignation of slaves."[1]

Or consider in this connection the implications of Luther's dictum that "Aside from faith, there is no reason for not living like swine." This means that but for religious belief, human and animal conduct are identical; man, then, finds in God the principles of humanity. But, replies Feuerbach, one is not in truth a man unless he considers humanity as the essential definition of his nature, as the essential character of his being. But why have we to go to God for principles of right human conduct if this is true? Are not the principles to be found, rather, in the character and essential nature of man's being?

A religious morality represses only the effects of moral evil, but not the causes; it hinders the manifestations of barbarism, but it does not cure them. A humanist morality, on the other hand, seeks the roots of morality, amorality, or immorality exclusively in humanity. And, in the last analysis, all morality proves its human origin. To illustrate: In former times men only observed the most elementary rules of hygiene and cleanliness in order to execute the commandments of God. To-day those same precepts seem rather childish to us; we execute them as a matter of course, and through human, rather than divine, impulsion. We conform to them naturally. Similarly, men of the future may be astonished in their time to know that we in our time only conduct ourselves morally out of deference to a superior, transcendent order. What we call moral conduct they may well call simply natural conduct.

[1] Lévy, op. cit., p. 165.

Let us turn, for a moment, to analysis of moral acts themselves. What we call an act truly moral in principle is spontaneous, unreflective, and uncommanded. No fiat from on high, no Kantian categorical imperative produces it. Just as the rules of rhetoric and syntax have never *produced* a literary masterpiece, so moral laws have never engendered moral acts. "True virtue is a natural child, a love child. What one ordinarily calls virtue is only an imitation, a copy which does not have the original value of life."[1] Take, for example, a woman who enjoys social life, bridge parties, and other such time-fillers. These occupations are in no sense immoral in themselves. But if this woman were to neglect her children and her home in order to attend teas, then her actions would be considered immoral by her neighbours who do take care of their homes and families. But the act of taking care of children is not moral in itself; it is, on the contrary, a natural tendency. Witness the millions of mothers who do it unreflectively, naturally, among them Christians, Mohammedans, atheists, socialists, and even "immoral" women. Duty is not something which comes from another world; it belongs to the same category as our drives and tendencies. "It is a natural instinct which expresses itself against the oppression of another instinct; remorse is the irritated shade, the 'spirit' of an instinct which a stronger instinct has murdered."[2]

But, it is asked, how have men come to think of duty as something outside themselves, as something supernatural? There are two answers. If duty were in no sense immanent, man would be deaf to its call, for it would be speaking to him in an ununderstood language. And, secondly, we come

[1] Lévy, op. cit., p. 168. [2] Ibid., pp. 168–9.

to exteriorize the idea of duty or the moral law in the same way in which we have exteriorized our gods. Duty is a manifestation of human nature, a consequence, in fact, of human nature. This consequence has only come to be considered autonomous, an *a priori* principle, in the course of civilization, as man has forgotten the origin of all things. "The moral man has first been carried or pushed in a determined direction; he has accepted this direction and made it the norm of his conduct; then he has imposed under the name of 'duty' to the man who succeeds him that which he had erected as law for himself, taking as point of departure the half true, half false idea that his successor is completely like himself.[1]"

In this analysis we see that the duty or moral law which prescribes any particular course of action is only man's tendency or penchant to that course of action raised to objectivity. These tendencies in themselves, from their origin, are technically amoral;* it is only when the just-outlined relatively unconscious process commences that the ideas of morality and immorality are brought into play.

But, adds Feuerbach, when an individual acts in a given manner without any inclination, uniquely through duty, he acts on a level no better than an animal level, by command. It is precisely because this artificial imitation obliges man to make an effort that he attributes certain merit to it and that he pretends to a transcendent recompense, immortality. Spontaneous, unreflective, naïve virtue, on the other hand, knows no merit and pretends to no inscrutable

---

[1] Lévy, op. cit., p. 170.

* Just as we speak, largely, about the amoral actions of a child or of an adult held to be mentally ill.

sanctions. The transcendent moralist, however, is unhappy in respect to such natural inclinations as he feels obliged to thwart in this life; he aspires to a hereafter in which life will be freer—not from licence, but from temptation. In that sense he hopes to be delivered in the future life from the yoke under which he labours in this. "But why make a false and lying virtue reign on earth, since, finally, in heaven, we will give free rein to our desires? Let us, from this time henceforth, harmonize our will and our sensibility."[1]

Only philistines who have no faith in the intrinsic worth of the nature of man conclude that this ethic makes way for licentiousness. True, it is Feuerbach's contention that it is not necessary, in order to assure harmonious social living, to refuse expression to natural tendencies. It is sufficient if each one be accorded its part of liberty in allowing the general interest of society to predominate.* For there exists between our natural social will and our penchants and drives the same relation as between species and individuals or between reason and sense. The savage who, without taking thought of the consequences, eats until he has nothing more to eat, is a slave of his own greediness. The civilized man, in taking account of his earthly future, apportions his enjoyments and thus eats only what he requires at the moment. The future, for him, is not supersensible. His awareness of it, and his conduct with reference to it, are completely human; his natural will permits him to elevate

[1] Lévy, op. cit., p. 170.
* This general position, in its social aspect, is akin to that of Mill. cf. his "Each man is free to do whatsoever he wills provided that, in so doing, he infringes not the equal freedom of another."

himself beyond his present desire. At its base, then, the antithesis between duty and inclination is only the translation into ethical terms of the opposition between the general and the particular.

Counterpose this position to that of Kant. The latter founds his ethic on the pure and absolute moral law. This to Feuerbach is the emptiest of procedures. "Form without matter is sterile; pure virtue is the mystery of the Immaculate Conception translated into the abstract language of Protestantism."[1] This whole attempt is simply to reduce Christianity to morality in order to rescue from supernaturalism all matters bordering on the practical. In trying to make morality the core of Christianity, Kant is doing just what Aristotle did to Greek paganism when he reduced the role of the gods to a theoretical one, making them objects of speculative intelligence. Kant's moral God is little but the personification of the moral law. For just as the general idea of any particular subject is not that subject in reality, so Kant's moral God is but the idea of moral actions and thus possesses solely the quality of a description of reality, but not reality itself. In attaching value to the form, rather than the content, of the law, Kant is obliged to admit a faculty uniquely determined by the law. This faculty is liberty.

We have not here the space to treat in detail Feuerbach's evolution of the idea of liberty. At the outset he rejected Kant's liberty, derived from the moral law, and Fichte's liberty, derived from the Self. These concepts he characterized as being too narrow in their definition of liberty as but an attribute of spirit, conceived in opposition to nature.

---

[1] Lévy, op. cit., p. 173.

Schelling, Feuerbach contends, had put the discussion on the right track in seeking the seed of liberty in nature itself,* although his definition had excluded order or law. In this sense he had turned too far away in the other direction. It was the merit of Hegel, then, in defining liberty as intellectual, to resolve the extremes of Kant and Schelling. But he neglected the subjective aspect of liberty.† In reviewing these doctrines in some detail, Feuerbach finally (in the tenth volume of his collected works) comes to this conclusion: The true liberty is happiness.

According to Feuerbach the whole history of religious ethics supports this thesis. Religions have imposed upon man certain duties in order better to insure his happiness; their laws have been consecrations of man's desires. Particularly in so far as man's ultimate desires have been unknown to him, has it been deemed necessary for his fellows who have preceded him to express their final judgment about the things most worth-while on this earth in such a form that these judgments would be conserved for posterity. The conflict between immediate and more ultimate goods has also been at the root of the problem. To prevent the immediate goods which might be destructive of ultimate goods from carrying off a victory over the latter, the general good has been objectivated into an ethic. Even in such cases as a given ethic might seem to point in the diametrically opposite direction from happiness, we find that, within the

* cf. Schelling's "Even the bit of dust on which you tread is animated with the divine breath of liberty; it has the sensation, if not the idea, of liberty."

† In his major critique of Hegel which we mentioned in the first chapter, Feuerbach reproaches Hegel for not having seen in creation an act of love.

limits of the given social situation, the basic ideal is still eudaemonistic. Thus, for example, even the ethic of Buddhism—although far from the ideal of an Epicurus or an Aristotle—expresses the most real ideal of happiness possible for the majority of individuals to whom the ethic at the time of its formulation might apply. If the notion of Nirvana seems a bit pessimistic to us, it is because the social situation under which this *summum bonum* was evolved made no other conception meaningful. To the first Buddhists, then, for whom this life was a vale of misery bathed in tears, a terminal *néant* was as blissful as are drug injections or anaesthetics to the suffering body of a sick man.

Feuerbach thus concludes that, if one consider an individual or a group in isolation, the individual or group has no other duty than that of assuring its own conservation and satisfying its egoism. The only qualification to this egoism stems from social living, which subordinates certain egoisms in co-ordinating egoisms in the aggregate. Disinterestedness and unselfishness, then, are created by the interest of others. And it is only in our relations with others that what we call conscience first comes into play. It is "the voice inside of us which is the echo of clamours from without."[1] Evil conscience is sympathy associated with the sting of knowing ourselves to have caused the unhappiness of a sufferer. Its presupposition is that man is able to feel his fellow's impulse toward happiness. It thus arises only in a social context; morality is a meaningless term with reference to single individuals; man is only man in society. Just as a physical birth requires two people, so the birth of morality requires more than an individual in isolation.

[1] Lévy, op. cit., p. 180.

It is, from the beginning, in the relation of the sexes that nature has accomplished the transition from the drive of the ego to a recognition of duty towards others. The sexual relation is, it might be said, the very basis of morality, for it is in this relation that isolated striving for happiness becomes a two- or more-sided striving. Here the fact becomes most patent that duties to oneself are indirect duties toward others.

Physical influences commence limiting the absolute power of the human ego from the very birth—pre-natally, in fact, according to Feuerbach—of the individual. Social experiences continue this limiting process. Thus as an individual becomes conscious of his own ego he also becomes conscious of that of others. This fact is well demonstrated by what Feuerbach considers to be one of the few thoroughly unhypocritical New Testament precepts, "Do unto others as you would have them do unto you." It expresses a psycho-genetically sound and fundamental truth. As such, it is completely moral in the Feuerbachian sense. And, to be sure, to the extent to which it is the latter, it is not a moral precept in the transcendental sense.

The result of the foregoing is a sort of eudaemonist Christian ethic, i.e. thou shalt love thy neighbour,* for only by so doing can you make both yourself and your neighbour happy. But do not expect to love him unselfishly, because, to the extent to which you are unselfish, you have no ego; the latter is necessary in order that you may really

---

* This Feuerbachian moral conclusion has often been compared to Comte's *Vive pour autrui* ("Live for one another"). Comte's ethic, however, starts with society; while Feuerbach's starts with the individual who seeks his completion in another and only comes, in the last analysis, to act for the whole by personal affection.

love your neighbour. Sympathy and human love presuppose that the person feeling them has himself experienced the need of happiness. Completely suppress egoism
and you suppress compassion. But do not worry, not having
suppressed egoism, for fear of selfishness run rampant. For
the very nature of the ego is communally human. Thus the
most egoistic being is the most compassionate. The Feuerbachian ethic, then, is eudaemonist. But its eudaemonism
is not the end, but the presupposition, of morality.

The Feuerbachian ethic, as we have reviewed it, demonstrates certain inconsistencies. In first formulating his ethic,
Feuerbach makes of love an unqualified good and of Egoism
an unqualified evil. Later on he tends to leave the problem
of evil completely behind and concentrate his interest and
analysis on the natural human qualities of the good. Had
he lived longer, his analysis might have been more complete. Such historians of philosophy as Höffding,[1] for
example, find his earlier writings too eudaemonistic but
admit, after reading Feuerbach's last fragments on the
problem, collected and published after his death by Grün,
that Feuerbach was on his way to establishing an ethic of
indisputable merit from the point of view of ethical systems.
For our part, we make no claims for Feuerbach as a moral
philosopher in the systematic sense. What we do insist,
however, is that Feuerbach was a worthy successor to the
French moralists of the school of Helvétius,* that he was
able for the first time to fit a generally eudaemonist ethic

[1] cf. his *History of Modern Philosophy*, translated by B. E. Meyer,
London, 1900, vol. ii, p. 282.

* Although, to be sure, Feuerbach himself disagreed basically with
Helvétius on many points. Witness his *Contra Helvetium*, among his last
papers collected by Grün.

into German philosophical surroundings, and that he laid much of the important groundwork for the ethics of the future. His major merit was to have seen that good and evil are not extrinsic, dual, transcendent principles, but rather completely natural principles, developmental, evolutionary, and intrinsic in nature and society.

*　　*　　*　　*　　*

It is with the last of our four categories, metaphysics, that we shall now concern ourselves.

A modern historian says that "the question what presuppositions underlie the physics or natural science of a certain people at a certain time is as purely historical a question as what kinds of clothes they wear. . . . And this is the question that metaphysicians have to answer. It is not their business to raise the further question whether, among the various beliefs on this subject that various peoples hold and have held, this one or that one is true."[1] One may be pardoned for wondering, if the latter is not the metaphysician's business, exactly whose business it is. Presumably either nobody's or history's; the author of the quotation is not quite explicit. On the other hand, it is true that metaphysics too often has seen everything but itself in perspective. For this reason, we make no pretension to finality in our assessment of Feuerbach's metaphysic. We shall try to treat the latter in the same spirit in which we would describe and analyse his wardrobe. Hegel, we submit, would have approved.

Feuerbach was highly critical of metaphysical speculation. In one passage, using the word "esoteric" in a rather

[1] R. G. Collingwood, *An Autobiography*, London, 1939, p. 66.

pejorative sense, he says that "Metaphysics are esoteric psychology."[1] It is his further contention that "Metaphysics or logic is only a real immanent science when it is not separated from subjective mind."[2] Feuerbach's general objections here are those we have already noted in his critique of philosophical idealism, noted in our first chapter. The flight from sense experience, the consequent separation of qualities from things, infinitude from finitude, indeterminateness from the determined, have created the split universe which is the chief preoccupation of metaphysics. Feuerbach rejects a qualitative difference between Fichte's Self or Ego and his own empirical self. He denies that Hegel's absolute Mind is anything more than an individual finite mind envisioned macroscopically and divorced from its specific, but not general, context. In short, Feuerbach sees no necessity in the metaphysical hiatus. In rejecting the dichotomy he rejects traditional metaphysics. He is, in this sense, no metaphysician.

But this does not mean that metaphysics in its simplest sense cannot ask questions about Feuerbach. Is he materialist or idealist? What is the status of man, soul, space, time, in this philosophy? These are significant questions for us.

Let us take the question of Feuerbach as a materialist, for it is this that he is generally labelled by historians of philosophy. In one sense he is a materialist; but it is not in this sense that he is generally considered so, but, rather, in several others. He is considered a materialist because of his anthropological approach to the philosophy of religion; he is considered a materialist in his rejection of speculative metaphysics. But it is just here, in answer to the historians,

---

[1] Feuerbach, *Sämmtliche Werke*, vol. ii, p. 248.   [2] Ibid., p. 248.

that Feuerbach would say he was an idealist, in a very special sense.* In any case, one thing is certain: Feuerbach's refutation of metaphysical materialism is no absolute idealism. It is in his 1838 essay in criticism of the materialism of Dorguth† that we will see his answer to the doctrine of static—as contrasted with dialectical—materialism. Let us follow his argument.

"We must," says Feuerbach, "object to the proposition 'thought is an activity of the brain'—a proposition which is fundamental to his (Dorguth's) writing and which does not mean that thinking is *also* a brain activity but that it is *only* a brain activity, the essence of thought, thought *in puris naturalibus*. . . . This proposition appears to us, if not exactly brainless, completely meaningless on the simple ground that so long as the brain is not itself mind, the activity of the mind must as such be a senseless activity. Consequently to characterize thought as a brain activity is to characterize the activity of thought as senseless."[1] Feuerbach's first criticism of this materialism, then, is that the analysis of thought as simply material activity is fatuous. Thought, he contends, must be understood in its own terms, through its specific activity and consequences, before one can pretend to analyse and control it solely through the conditions in which it takes place. If we cannot at the outset successfully make this distinction, then we will never be able to make the necessary distinction between matter and one's idea of matter. Secondly, if thought is a

* "I am an idealist," he wrote, ". . . in the region of practical philosophy." cf. *The Essence of Christianity*, p. viii.

† Expressed in the latter's *Kritik des Idealismus*.

[1] Feuerbach, *Sämmtliche Werke*, vol. ii, p. 139.

product of the brain in the same way that bile is a product of the liver,* then why is it not as tangible in relation to the brain as is the bile which flows from the liver? "If it is unreal then it is an unreal product and there is nothing but brain, no thought; if it is real, then we can no more apply the distinction of true and false to ideas than we can to the brain."[1] Feuerbach, as a case in point, dares the absolute materialist to take the thoughts of an idealist. According to the materialist theory, the idealist's ideas are a product of the material conditions under which thought takes place; there is an ineluctable direct rapport between the idealist's philosophical idealism and his brain. How, then, can these ideas be false, as the materialists say they are?

Absolute materialism, it follows, cannot deny the existence of thought, but only its independent efficacy. But if the latter is denied, the former must be denied also; it is impossible to assert the one and not the other; thought, in fact, is only known to us by its efficacy in making itself known. But how to explain this material priority rapport if the effects of thought can destroy their bodily cause as, for example, in suicide? Animals do not take their own lives, although like men they are subject to the laws of the material world around them. Then, demands Feuerbach, "Explain to me the death of the sage or the hero who stakes his head upon his ideas. Explain to me the power of ideas upon the organism if the idea is nothing but an excrescence of the organism."[2]

---

* cf. also the physiological materialism of Karl Vogt.

[1] Hook, op. cit., p. 239. Who, if the point needs to be further driven home, would say that bile is either true or false? It simply *is*.

[2] Feuerbach, op. cit., p. 146.

Another point. In rejecting the reality of ideas, the absolute materialists can only utilize the concept of pure, direct, unmediated sense-experience as the conveyor of knowledge. But this means that materialists cannot be scientists; they cannot anticipate experience. The hypothetical thinking that takes place in scientific practice has no connection with the direct sense perceptions which we have of the objects with which science is concerned. That is why science is different from, say, history. Furthermore, if we understood solely on the basis of direct sense experience, whence would arise epistemological error? Here Feuerbach cites the example of the Copernican revolution, the essential conclusions of which completely violated the knowledge given by the senses. "O! Nicholas Copernicus," he says, "be happy that you have not lived in our times, in this age of spiritual degradation, historicism, empiricism, and positivism. Had you only now come forward with such a daring and heroic *apriorism*, you would, at least, have been obliged to atone for your idealistic chimera in a madhouse."[1]

Here, lest one think that the consequence of the above means a return to Kant, we must explain that by *a priori* Feuerbach does not mean independent of experience. He rather identifies it with the power of the understanding, as an exigency of thought. "To pass judgment upon objects of experience independently of experience is nonsense; if a philosopher ever pretended to possess or convey *a priori* knowledge in this sense, he was a fool. . . . The idea of sense phenomena . . . is *a priori*, the only *a priori*."[2]

The preceding is the outline of Feuerbach's declaration of independence from metaphysical or systematic mate-

[1] Feuerbach, op. cit., p. 144.   [2] Feuerbach, op. cit., p. 151.

rialism. True, certain aspects of the position he here criticizes he himself adopts in later years,* but never the position *in toto.* "Nature for him always retained an intelligible pattern even when he was not sure whether its intelligibility was an object of the understanding or an object of sensation."[1] Those who simply dismiss Feuerbach as a vulgar materialist† should, we submit, seriously consider the aspect of Feuerbachianism here revealed.

It is in another sense that Feuerbach may be discriminately called a materialist, *via* his naturalism. In an exceedingly comprehensive paper delivered before the American Philosophical Association[2] a few years ago, Dr. Sidney Hook sought to arrive at a definitive statement of the position of materialism *vis-à-vis* other philosophical attitudes. We have not here the space to undertake a review of his analysis. Suffice to say that, after discussing all the historical and actual differences between materialism and idealism, Hook finds that the real difference can be boiled down to that between naturalism and supernaturalism. Assuming this to be true, Feuerbach must be classed among materialists and so must, for example, Comte. While this departure from traditional labels might be convenient for purposes of discriminate analysis, the fact remains that Hook's definition—which, we submit, is far more meaningful than the traditional definitions—not having been propounded a century ago, can be used but with difficulty in

---

* Particularly in his extreme sensationalism, inspired by Moleschott, which we have already discussed.

[1] Hook, op. cit., p. 242.

† To be uncritically lumped with Büchner, Vogt, and Moleschott.

[2] Published in the American *Journal of Philosophy*, April 1934, under the title *What is Materialism?*

connection with problems and attitudes to which other labels have so long been applied.

In discussing the metaphysical approach to Feuerbachianism, there is one other particular classic philosophical problem which here poses itself. It has been one of the more crucial ontological problems throughout the history of philosophy. It is the question to which the answers of nominalism and realism have been delivered. What is the relation between the laws of thought and the laws of things?

Feuerbach nowhere deals very explicitly with this problem. It is one of the more speculative nuts which philosophers have spent so long a time in cracking that Feuerbach concluded, it seems, that it was not worth while wasting time with. In so far as he does deal with the question collaterally his answer is, in our judgment, an unequivocally weak point in his philosophy. For the general anthropocentric orientation of his philosophy would, we contend, necessitate a complete nominalism. It is the implication of his humanism that laws and principles are man-made, socially determined; that they are simple exigencies of thought, if you will, as uniformly pervasive as human reason,* but not having any independent objective status. To some extent Feuerbach is faithful to this implication.† But only to some extent, for when he finds himself

---

* cf. Feuerbach's "Human beings have only one, or only one common, Reason; because they have only one, or common, nature and organization."—Grün, op. cit., vol. i, p. 393.

† So faithful, in fact, that, according to Hook, Marx and Engels were considerably bothered about it. "Engels seems worried lest the laws by which bridges are built be transformed into convenient constructions of humanity."—Hook, op. cit., p. 265.

face to face with the problem he says "The laws of reality are also laws of thought,"[1] strictly a realist answer: universals have the same independent objective existential status as things.

And when, for example, he writes about space and time, he seems to consider them virtually noumenal beings. We have seen this, to some extent, in Feuerbach's description of sensation and existence in his initial answer to the question of personal immortality. Here is his answer, even more explicitly stated, in a rather humorous letter to Taillandier: "Please know, sir, that in my philosophy—which knows no gods and which, consequently, admits no miracles in the domain of politics, in my doctrine, of which you know and understand almost nothing, although you pretend to judge me, rather than studying me—space and time are the fundamental conditions of all existence and all being, of all thought and all action, of all progress and all success. It is not because belief in God is lacking in Parliament, as has been so ridiculously maintained in the Chamber of the council of Bavaria—the majority of deputies are believers, and the good God, in taking his decisions, also doubtless takes into account the majority;—it is because the sense of place and time is lacking, that it finishes so pitifully without giving results."[2]

In thus giving a realist answer to the chief ontological problem Feuerbach is, to a large extent, inconsistent with the human orientation of his philosophy. On the other hand, he obviously saw the consequences inherent in a

[1] Feuerbach, op. cit., p. 334.

[2] Feuerbach, *Sämmtliche Werke*, vol. viii, Introduction; quoted by Lévy, op. cit., p. 46.

purely nominalist sensationalism; he criticized them in his criticism of Dorguth's absolute materialist epistemology and ontology. It is Feuerbach's realism which saves him from an extreme sensationalism in which neither prediction nor verification would be possible. He does it by means of "the characters of unity and difference given our senses," which we dealt with discussing sensationalism. The problem is a knotty one; we do not pretend that Feuerbach's half-solution is free from contradiction. For these characters of unity and difference given our senses must either be independently given, in which case our complete and exclusive human orientation is last and we have to postulate at least a logico-metaphysical quality of permanent objective validity, thereby opening the door to transcendence; or else they are themselves products of experience, given to our senses in a manner not heretofore analysed, and we have a sort of dualism extant inside the sensibly given. In avoiding the Scylla of super-sensationalism, which might lead to solipsism, we seem to have piled up on the Charybdis of external objectivity, which might lead back to the transcendence which we were trying to steer clear of in the first place.*

The preceding difficulty is pointed out, not to try to

* It is of collateral interest to note that those who have tried to track this problem down from the exclusive viewpoint of logic find the same difficulty. Thus Dewey, in his *Logic, a Theory of Inquiry* (New York, 1938) builds a logic from the ground up, using only empirical tools, and finds in the end that certain principles—i.e. the Aristotelian laws of identity, non-contradiction, and excluded middle—which seem to have other than completely empirical points of repair, must be admitted. Whether the classification of these simply as exigencies of thought avoids our dilemma is a question, the last word on which has by no means been said.

cover up Feuerbach's inadequate and contradictory answer to the nominalist-realist question, but to show that the problem is a crucial one, no definitive resolution of which has, in our estimation, been arrived at.

What, in conclusion, can be said about Feuerbach's metaphysic? He is not, strictly speaking, a materialist or an idealist with reference to the fundamental cosmological questions. He is metaphysically a humanist. Man and the world are to the materialist the result of matter in motion; man and the world are to the idealist the result of an absolute Self or Mind; man and the world are to Feuerbach the *result* of nothing; he *starts* with them. Such problems as the final ground of knowledge, the origin of evil, the nature and the destiny of the soul, are inside, not outside, man. Just as Hegelianism leaves nothing outside reason, no insoluble remainder, so Feuerbachianism leaves nothing outside humanity; even its unsolved and sometimes contradictory aspects are inside man. Similarly, one can apply the same dictum to such questions as one may think Feuerbach did not, but should have, answered, as Croce applies to those same questions with reference to Hegel: "The questions to which philosophy has no answer have their answer in this, *that they ought not to be asked.*"[1]

We conclude. Feuerbach's metaphysic echoes down the long canyon of philosophy the challenge flung forth by Pope from atop the not always magic mountain of poetry:

"Know Thyself; presume not God to scan.
The proper study of mankind is man."

[1] Croce, op. cit., p. 71.

Chapter VI

FEUERBACH AND MARX

It is not our intention in this chapter to discuss the philosophy of Karl Marx. But, just as it is impossible to commence a discussion of the philosophy of Feuerbach without mentioning Hegel, so it is impossible to terminate it without reference to Marx. For Marx was, in the three or four most crucial years of his development, a Feuerbachian.

The points at which Marxism and Feuerbachianism impinge upon one another have been touched upon by implication several times throughout this book. In general, it might be said that it was Feuerbach's principled flight from transcendence which blazed the trail for Marxism. In more specific terms, it was what Hook has called Feuerbach's "theory of the natural fetishism of human activity" which was the rallying point for Marx and others among the Young Hegelian rebels. For, they concluded, "If the religious fact *par excellence* is the alienation of man from himself, the erection of a *product* of man's own emotional and intellectual activity into an objective norm claiming *a priori* validity, then it could be shown that the whole of society was pervaded by a religious principle."[1] And this is just what

[1] Hook, op. cit., pp. 248–9.

Marx proceeded to do, extending the general Feuerbachian formula to admittedly secular aspects of human culture, to economics and politics. Feuerbach's ethical principles were translated into political terms to show that the state exists for man, rather than the Hegelian vice versa. Feuerbach had shown the baselessness of the whole idea of religious heresy; the idea of political heresy was analogously shown to be baseless. Feuerbach had keenly analysed the dualism between the sacred and the profane which institutional religion had imported into social living; an analogue to this dualism appeared in the separation of political from economic responsibility in the state. And in consonance with Feuerbach's theoretical humanism, which was his answer to the religious and philosophical problem which confronted him, the Marxists posed a practical humanism as answer to the socio-economic problem in which they saw the major determinant of all other problems.

We may be permitted here to take two typical quotations, the one reflecting Feuerbach's philosophy of religion and the other reflecting his general metaphysical position, in demonstration of Marx's initial Feuerbachianism: Says Marx, "The organs of the political state are religious by virtue of the dualism between the life of bourgeois society and political life—religious, in that man regards the transcendental life of the state which is so foreign to his real individuality as his true life, religious in so far as religion is the spirit of bourgeois society, the expression of the separation and division of man from man."[1] Compare this with any of Feuerbach's dicta on the hiatus between man's real, natural self, and his self-alienation, repository both

[1] Marx, *Gesamtausgabe*, vol. i, p. 590; quoted Hook, op. cit., p. 250.

of his values and the fancies which are in his natural life denied him.

And compare the following with Feuerbach's metaphysical position as discussed in the last chapter: "A consistently carried out naturalism or humanism distinguishes itself from idealism as well as materialism and at the same time unifies what is true in both. We can also see that only naturalism is capable of grasping the acts of world history."[1]

These two quotations may serve to give some indication of Marx's early Feuerbachianism.* This is important both for an understanding of historical materialism as a system and for an understanding of the Marxian theory of the state. For, as Marx said, "It is the philosopher in whose brain the revolution is beginning."[2]

Upon such relatively rare occasions as present-day Marxists read Feuerbach, their principal criticism of him is that he was unable to tie down his human insights to concrete social reality; and that, in rejecting the Hegelian dialectic, he had no real conception of the sweep of history, no implement with which to treat the movement and development of thought and the social context in which it takes place. This criticism does, in short, resolve itself into a plaint that Feuerbach was not Marx. Let us see briefly to what extent it is justified.

It is indubitably true that Feuerbach was not a socio-

[1] Quoted by Hook, op. cit., p. 272.

* Explicit detailed tribute to Feuerbach can be found both in Marx's *The Holy Family*, written on behalf of "real humanism," and in *The German Ideology*, in the first section of which Marx defends Feuerbach against the attacks of Bruno Bauer and Stirner.

[2] Marx, Engels, *The German Ideology*, London, 1938, p. xi.

logist, as was his contemporary Comte, or a social philosopher, as was Marx. He was primarily interested in man's regaining of his own essence, and came to consider society only because—not unlike Plato, who could analyse virtue better in the state than in the individual—he found the essence of humanity in man in the aggregate. But the conditions of aggregate existence are not always important to him. This point is well illustrated by a part of his discussion on immortality in *The Essence of Christianity*. Discussing the imagined beatitude of the future life, Feuerbach finds extraordinary support for his thesis that the imagined hereafter is but a special objectified reflection of our present life in the dying words of a negro slave who refused baptismal inauguration to immortality with these words: "I don't want another life, boss, not at all; for I'd probably be your slave there, too."[1] But he does not see in this the important social picture: The slave's master and the priest on the one side, the slave on the other. The way in which this relation has implemented and perpetuated immortality ideas does not interest Feuerbach. He only rejoices that the slave has not so alienated himself as to lose perspective, that he has kept enough of his own essence to realize that an imagined hereafter would not be all milk and honey, or even, to bring the figure up to date, beer and skittles.

On the other hand, Feuerbach demonstrates in certain of his aphorisms that the importance of the relation between religion and a given particular social situation is not unknown to him. Take, for example, this aphorism: "What is the most certain sign that a religion no longer possesses

---

[1] From Parny, *Œuvres Choisies*, Paris, 1827; quoted by Feuerbach, *The Essence of Christianity*, p. 179.

in itself any vital force? It is when one sees the princes of the world offer it the aid of their arms to put it back on its feet."[1] It is our contention that Feuerbach here saw the truth of the fact that religion's vital force varies in direct proportion to its degree of social and political rebelliousness. True, he thought this situation would, in a large measure, be progressively cleared up by the separation of Church and State,* but, then, so did Marx and Engels during their early period.

Feuerbach is criticized by Marxists for having, in his critique of Hegel, emptied out the baby with the bath water; in disposing of the systematic idealism of Hegel he also rejected the rational kernel of Hegel's method, the dialectic. It is true that Feuerbach never mentions dialectics, but we demur at the criticism that there are not even traces of the Hegelian dialectic in his philosophy. Feuerbach's religious systole and diastole, while not formally dialectical, are at least materially so; man is the thesis, his self-alienation the antithesis, and Feuerbach's ideal of humanity a synthesis.

But, it will immediately be objected, Feuerbach wanted a return to the thesis, not a higher synthesis. We disagree. Feuerbach sought only to explain man's natural fetishism, not to destroy it; the latter is impossible, on the very Feuerbachian ground that the fetishism is natural. Feuerbach only wants us to be aware of that which we have done unconsciously, that we may recapture our essence. The

[1] Feuerbach's *Religion from the Point of View of Anthropology*, Roy edition, p. 346.

* At numerous points in Feuerbach's writing we see hopeful reference to the future of humanity in the United States, where religion is constitutionally a private matter.

formula is: Man plus self-alienation equals recaptured essence. The recaptured essence is a synthesis, not a direct return to the thesis. This latter would be true only if men were animals.*

Another Feuerbachian unacknowledged use of the dialectic occurs in his treatment of the natural life of man, as we have observed it in our discussion of immortality. He shows how the creative penchant of nature is also a destructive penchant, how each new degree of life is the death of that which precedes it. The very process of growth, he avers, is the birth of new forms on top of the death of old. The child does not evolve into the youth; the child dies, and out of his death arises the youth. What is this if not the negation of the negation? Feuerbach's whole discussion here might, with certain emendations, have been lifted out of his *Werke* and placed in the thirteenth chapter of *Anti-Dühring*.[1]

Feuerbach does not make explicit use of the Hegelian dialectic. He does, however, consciously or unconsciously use it in part, and in a comprehensive manner. His use of it is a worthy introduction to the brilliant transformation and use of it which was made subsequently by Marx and Engels.

Furthermore, in considering Marx's and Engels' relation to Feuerbach, let us rid ourselves once and for all of the notion that the entire doctrine of Marxism, armoured and with sword in hand, sprung from Marx's head one afternoon. Marxism, Topsy, and Marx have this one thing in common,

---

* cf. our initial discussion on the essential nature of man, in chapter ii.

[1] cf. Engels, *Anti-Dühring*, English ed., London, Martin Lawrence, chapter xiii on "Dialectics: The Negation of the Negation."

that they "growed". Engels is highly critical of Feuerbach's neglect of what was truly living in Hegelianism, in his brochure on Feuerbach written in 1888, some forty-five years after his own Feuerbachian youth. He had doubtless forgotten his own and Marx's state of mind during the time that their doctrine was being formulated. But listen to Marx's early praise of Feuerbach for the latter's demolition of Hegelianism: "Who has put an end to the dialectic of concepts, to the war of the gods, that the philosophers alone knew? Feuerbach. Who has placed man in the stead of the former rubbish, driving away with the same stroke the infinite conscience? Feuerbach, Feuerbach alone."[1] And Engels, too, was decidedly Feuerbachian at the outset. In his *Outline of a Critique of Political Economy*, he compares the history of political economy to the history of theology. The mercantile system is the Catholic Middle Ages of commerce; the free-exchange economy of Adam Smith corresponds to liberal Protestantism. Just as theology can neither turn back to blind faith nor proceed onwards to free philosophy, so can free-exchange economy neither turn back to feudalism nor proceed onwards to the suppression of individual ownership of the property of production. Engels finds that true relations in economy are reversed, just as Feuerbach had found that true relations in theology are reversed. Value is made to depend upon price; this inversion, remarks Engels, is the essence of abstraction. Furthermore, Engels uses a Feuerbachian formula for human conduct when he enjoins workers to "Produce with conscience, as men, not as dispersed atoms without collective conscience; this is the only way to remedy social

[1] Mehring, *Nachlass*, vol. ii, p. 197.

crises and the profound degradation of man."[1] Engels did, in the course of time, considerably qualify this dictum, but it was, we submit, his Feuerbachianism which set him on the track in the first place.

But it is not our intention here to engage in a polemic in defence of Feuerbach. He stands on his own feet. We only seek, rather, to show that the Feuerbachian elements in the lives and thought of Marx and Engels were important, and that at least some of those elements specifically came to pervade the structure of Marxism.

Lévy* says that "at the moment they met, Marx and Engels were both Feuerbachians without reserve; their ideal was to realize humanity in organizing society. . . . If both of them counted on the revolutionary action of the proletariat, neither of them yet spoke about the class struggle. The proletariat, they thought, will realize humanity because it is on the one hand the most unfortunate class, the class most dehumanized by the present state of affairs, and on the other hand the most open to philosophic thought, the most human in spirit."[2] Even after Marx and Engels had proclaimed their definitive class teleology and the separate structure of historical materialism had been built, the Feuerbachian elements in it could still be seen. One of the most rigorous of dialectical materialist formulas, that which broadly defines the human conscience as a mirror of socio-economic facts, comes from *The Essence of Christianity*.

[1] cf. Mehring, *Nachlass*, vol. i, pp. 438–9.

* Lévy's chapter iii is a detailed and serious account of the Feuerbachian influences in Marxism. It does, we submit, tend to overstate the case, but this is explicable in the light of some of the later Marxist attacks on Feuerbach.

[2] Lévy, op. cit., pp. 275–6.

According to Feuerbach, God is the image of man; according to Marx, the sentiments and ideas of men are the reflections of the conditions of their existence. According to Feuerbach, the history of the gods is the celestial repetition of the earthly progress of men; according to Marx, human history is a reflection of the history of the conditions of production.

Having thus far noted the Feuerbachianism in Marxism, we must further note the meta-Feuerbachianism in Marxism. We shall do this in a short *résumé* of the salient criticisms of Feuerbach contained in Marx's *Theses on Feuerbach* and in Engels' *L. Feuerbach*. These serve, in our estimation, as a signpost in the history of philosophy, they indicate the parting of the ways. Feuerbach had been a surveyor; Marx and Engels were builders. The sub-title of Engels' brochure has been translated as "The Outcome of German Classical Philosophy." It may better be translated, we contend, "The Exit of German Classical Philosophy."*

First, Marx's theses.† These are eleven in number; they were written early in 1845, not for publication, but in Marx's notebook as private notes. They were subsequently published as appendices to *The German Ideology* and to Engels' *L. Feuerbach*. In the first three theses Marx characterizes the former materialism, in which he roughly includes Feuerbachianism, and idealism—both of them *vis-à-vis* historical materialism.

The chief defect in pre-Marxian materialism, Marx

* In the original German it is: *L. Feuerbach und der Ausgang der klassischen deutschen Philosophie.*

† For a thoroughly detailed analysis of the theses see Hook, op. cit., chapter viii.

asserts, is that the object or reality is conceived only in the form of the object of contemplation, but not as human activity, subjectively. The subjective side, by default, has been developed by idealism, but only abstractly. A synthesis of thought and being has not been arrived at, then, either by materialism or idealism, since both have imprisoned themselves within abstraction. The only way in which this synthesis can be arrived at, the only way to prove the reality of knowledge, is by practice. "The dispute over the reality or non-reality of thinking which is isolated from practice is a purely scholastic question."[1]

Ignoring nature and the role of human activity, the former, "vulgar," materialism considered man as a product of his environment and his education, without seeing that man's *milieu* is also transformed by him. The world does not exist independently of man; the educator educates, and the educator is educated. The relation between man and his world is always one of interaction.

So much for the first three theses. In the three following ones Marx shows the consequences of Feuerbach's socially detached attitude, itself stemming from the fact that Feuerbach was not aware of the principles involved in the first three theses. Feuerbach had started out with the fact of man's self-alienation in religion, of his duplication of the world into an imaginary and a real one. But Feuerbach does not seriously inquire into the *raison d'être* of this duplication. This latter is, says Marx, the expression of social contradictions which must be understood and suppressed if Feuerbach's ideal of the reintegration of man is to be

[1] Marx, Thesis II; in Appendix to Engels, *L. Feuerbach*, London, 1934, p. 73.

effected. "Thus, for instance, once the earthly family is discovered to be the secret of the holy family, the former must then itself be theoretically criticized and radically changed in practice."[1] Furthermore, in his analysis of religion, Feuerbach rejects abstract idealism and opposes to it the reality of the sensible world. But since he does not conceive this reality under the form of human activity, he is incapable of modifying it. Thus Feuerbach can only show us the origin of religion, but cannot do anything about the problems and predicaments he reveals. He is led to consider man in himself, an isolated being, outside social life and outside history. To Feuerbach man remains an abstraction; the essence of humanity, human collectivity, is to him but an ensemble of individuals who are not united by any social, but only by comparatively undefined internal ties. "The human essence, therefore, can with him be comprehended only as 'genus,' as a dumb internal generality which merely *naturally* unites the many individuals."[2]

From this point Marx goes on to show that as consequence Feuerbach does not see that the religious sentiment is itself a social product, and that the abstract individual whom he analyses is himself a member of a particular and definite form of society. Society has an essentially practical character; it is made up of the union of man with Nature, realized by human activity, especially economic activity. Only when we have understood the character of social life and human activity can the problems which incline men towards mysticism, and towards religious and social illusions be resolved. It is only historical materialism,

[1] Thesis IV, in Appendix to Engels, *L. Feuerbach*, p. 74.
[2] Thesis VI, ibid., p. 75.

concludes Marx, which, considering the true nature of man as constituted by his social activity, can raise itself above the notion of the isolated individual, as he exists in Hegelian civil society and as he is conceived by Feuerbach, and arrive at the true conception of collective being or socialized humanity. Henceforth the problem is to be found in a completely different area: "The philosophers have only *interpreted* the world in various ways; the point, however, is to *change* it."[1]

Thus does Marx mark the end of his exclusively Feuerbachian period, definitely establishing his doctrine of historical materialism, considering history as the processus of man's adaptation to his social environment, itself dominantly expressed by modes of production and of work. Herein is to be found the Marxian synthesis of man and nature.

These theses so comprehensively and definitely mark the meta-Feuerbachian aspect of Marxism that there is relatively little left to be said. Through them we understand why Feuerbach could only continue to spin his philosophy around the evils which come from the "head and the heart of man"—evils which, in a large measure, could be pointed out but not cured—while Marx and Engels could treat the whole man by starting, but by no means ending, with his stomach.

There are, however, two additional points about Feuerbachianism which stand out from Engels' extended restatement of the theses in his *L. Feuerbach*. The first concerns Feuerbach's materialism; the second, his ethics.

In the last section of the preceding chapter we discussed

---

[1] Thesis XI, in Appendix to Engels, *L. Feuerbach*, p. 75.

Feuerbach's metaphysic, concluding that in the naturalist *v.* supernaturalist sense it is materialist; but that in the history of philosophy it is justly not considered so, as the term materialist has been reserved for philosophies which construct the universe out of matter in motion. Engels defines the term in a less confusing sense. He points out that "By the word materialism the philistine understands gluttony, drunkenness, lust of the eye, lust of the flesh, arrogance, cupidity, avarice, miserliness, profit-hunting, and stock-exchange swindling—in short, all the filthy vices in which he himself indulges in private. By the word idealism he understands the belief in virtue, universal philanthropy and in a general way a 'better world,' of which he boasts before others, but in which he himself at the utmost believes only so long as he is going through the depression or bankruptcy consequent upon his customary 'materialist' excesses."[1]

Engels' definition directly revolves around the question as to whether a god created the world or whether it has been in existence eternally. Those who answer by asserting the primacy of spirit to nature and therefore assert some sort of world creation comprise the camp of idealism. Those who answer the question by asserting the primacy of nature to spirit comprise the camp of materialism. Feuerbach, then, in Engels' analysis, is a materialist. "Then came *The Essence of Christianity*," says Engels in an earlier passage. "With one blow it pulverized the contradiction, in that without circumlocutions it placed materialism on the throne again. Nature exists independently of all philosophy."[2]

This we mention to clear up the confusion which has

---

[1] Engels, op. cit., pp. 41–2. [2] Ibid., p. 28.

arisen from the fact that historians of philosophy have usually literally accepted Feuerbach's denial of materialism, and class him as a humanist or positivist; while Marxists, on the other hand, tend to regard him as one of the last, but not least, of the vulgar materialists.

In the last chapter we discussed Feuerbach's ethic, noting how he tries to fit eudaemonism into the German philosophical context. Engels here bitingly criticizes this ethic, asserting that "The Feuerbachian theory of morals fares like all its predecessors. It is designed to suit all periods, all peoples, and all conditions, and precisely for that reason it is never and nowhere applicable."[1] Engels compares the Feuerbachian ethic with that of Hegel, recognizing that the latter, at least, was historically meaningful, that the Hegelian incarnation of evil in the motive force of historical development could explain the moral facet of class antagonisms in history and show how the "wicked" passions of men are the levers of historical development. Feuerbach, on the other hand, sees morality out of history, and presupposes an objectivity by which the consequences of man's actions can be judged which does not, in fact, exist. Moreover, the ethic of love, which we have called in another connection the cement in the social structure, is not a desideratum to the Marxist, to whom a certain amount of dynamite in the social structure is an essential precondition to the proper reconstruction of our society whose present essential nature is such that no matter how much love be applied to it, the realization of socialized humanity is not possible within its framework.

Engels' further commentary needs no discussion—only

---

[1] Engels, op. cit., p. 50.

quotation. "According to Feuerbach's theory of morals the Stock Exchange is the highest temple of moral conduct provided only that one always speculates correctly. If my urge toward happiness leads me to the Stock Exchange, and if I there correctly gauge the consequences of my actions so that only agreeable results and no disadvantages ensue, that is, if I always win, then I am fulfilling Feuerbach's precept. Moreover, I do not thereby interfere with the equal right of another person to pursue his happiness; for that other man went to the Exchange just as voluntarily as I did and in concluding the speculative transaction with me he has followed his urge toward happiness as I have followed mine. Should he lose his money, then by that very fact his activity is proved to have been immoral, because of his bad reckoning, and since I have given him the punishment he deserves, I can even slap my chest proudly, like a modern Rhadamanthus. Love, too, rules on the Stock Exchange . . . for each finds in others the satisfaction of his own urge towards happiness. . . . And if I gamble with correct prevision of the consequences of my operations, and therefore with success, I fulfil all the strictest injunctions of Feuerbachian morality—and become a rich man into the bargain. In other words, Feuerbach's morality is cut exactly to the pattern of modern capitalist society, little as Feuerbach himself might imagine or desire it.

"But love! Yes, with Feuerbach, love is everywhere and at all times the wonder-working god who should help to surmount all difficulties of practical life—and that in a society which is split into classes with diametrically opposite interests. At this point the last relic of its revolutionary character disappears from the philosophy, leaving only the old cant: Love one another—fall into each other's arms regardless of distinctions of sex or estate—a universal orgy of reconciliation."[1]

The moral problem resolves itself into this: Philosophers before the advent of historical materialism had hypostatized ethical systems which pretended to universality. Hegel had largely cut the ground away from beneath such systems; Feuerbach's eudaemonism was a throw-back. The materialist systems after Feuerbach no longer laid claim to universality in ethics; Marxist ethics have been special ethics, deriving their authority from a particular social grouping and attested by the distinctive Marxist *praxis*, practice. Engels justly criticizes the Feuerbachian ethic in the light of the insights of developed Marxism; his very vehemence is a measure of his own former proximity to the Feuerbachian position. His is, to some extent, a criticism of Feuerbach for not having lived longer, as well as for not having seen differently. Yet one cannot help feeling that it was needlessly emphatic; Marx himself—although he passed beyond Feuerbach before 1850—was always conscious of his debt to Feuerbach; and even Engels does not upbraid Aristotle for not having envisioned the problems of the machine age!

Further, we submit, Engels should have paid greater attention to the role of the Feuerbachian principle of love in effecting the transition from a transcendent orientation to the human orientation. For it was just this principle, in its religious context, which had made the gods tenable in an age in which gods without love would have been instantly rejected. The placing of the principle in its human

[1] Engels, op. cit., pp. 49–50.

context avoided the necessity of a frontal attack on the gods; they simply and suddenly became, psychologically speaking, superfluous. It was just this demonstration of their superfluity which attracted so many spirits, among them Marx and Engels, to *The Essence of Christianity*. This individual liberation was, we submit, a necessary forerunner of the more general social liberation, the necessity of which first became patent to Marx and Engels through Feuerbach. All of which is in no way intended to deny the historic steps taken by Marx and Engels, steps which Feuerbach did not take; but is only intended to recall that there was another, earlier, step which they had to take, and which Feuerbach took before them.

*　　*　　*　　*　　*

The foregoing has served to make clear that Feuerbach, despite his bold self-definition as a communist, was not a communist in the Marxian, scientific sense. Feuerbach's very words in so characterizing himself are revealing. He says, in an answer to Stirner, "Feuerbach, you say, is not a materialist, idealist, or a believer in the philosophy of identity. Well, then, what is he? He is in thought as in deed, in spirit as in flesh, in essence as in feeling *man*; or, rather, since for him the essence of man is given only in society, communal man, Communist."[1] This is a statement to which the most respectable of the humanists of to-day can subscribe, be they humanist pastors or humanist bankers.

[1] Feuerbach, *Sämmtliche Werke*, vol. i, p. 342. It was this statement which once brought the police down upon Feuerbach's head, and caused his Bruckberg house to be officially searched for evidences of seditious activity.

There is nothing here in common with class-struggle communism. In fact, it is upon this passage that Marx, in *The German Ideology*, seizes to criticize the vagueness of Feuerbach's thought.

What, then, is Feuerbach? His philosophy did, to be sure, serve as inspiration and point of repair for the so-called German "true" or "philosophical" socialists,* against whom Marx polemized in the *Communist Manifesto*. But Feuerbach does not belong narrowly to any political group, religious sect, or philosophical fraternity. He lives to-day through Marxism which followed him; and he belongs to that in which he was, however unconcretely, most interested—humanity.

* For a characterization of true socialism see Cornu, *Moses Hess et la Gauche Hegélienne*, Paris, 1934; and Hook, op. cit., chapter vi.

L'ENVOI

The death of Hegel brought in its wake a period of uncertainty and confusion. Critical philosophy had failed; the cult of the State was leading to greater and greater social reaction; liberalism was uncertain in doctrine and hesitant in action; and the emerging philosophy of socialism increasingly appeared to be just another problem, rather than a solution. "In this confusion," says one commentator, "there was but one luminous point, one certitude: the theory of Feuerbach, which posed the problem of the synthesis of philosophical thought and practical action on the social level, on the level of concrete humanity, and which furnished the essential elements for a solution."[1]

This theory did not defend or attack religion; it simply explained it, thereby giving the *coup de grâce* to speculative literal theology. This theory gave to those* driven into opposition by a reactionary government new arms with which to fight back, against the Church and against a Prussia unfaithful to its progressive historic mission. This theory, in renouncing the transcendent hereafter and in cleaving to the earthly City, gave to political action a singular nobility; in showing that religion is but a manifestation of human ambition, an act of rebellion, an attempt to seize power and organize the universe, it conferred a

---

[1] Cornu, *Karl Marx, l'Homme et l'Œuvre*, Paris, 1934, p. 219.
* Arnold Ruge, *et al.*

religious title upon men of action, assuring them the spiritual heritage of the prophets. Its high critique of faith paved the way for a higher critique of law.

Lamentable but true, much of this is not the material of technical philosophy. But in the domain of the latter, also, Feuerbach's doctrine is of incontestable import. A leading historian of philosophy says that "in the history of German philosophy Feuerbach appears as the most energetic of the thinkers who effected the transition from Romantic speculation to critical self-comprehension, and returned afresh to the investigation of the first presuppositions of all our knowledge and all our estimation of worth."[1] In the philosophy of religion Feuerbach is still the master. On humanism, sensationalism, ethics, and metaphysics he has left his imprint.

Feuerbach made no social revolutions, built no churches, founded no schools; he is the object of devotion of no considerable number of people in our time. In what way, then, is he important to the philosophically uninitiated, to the man on the street to-day? He is important because he told us once again where new truth can be found: "Thou knowest that a new truth has ever come to the world with decorations and royal éclat, to the sound of drums and trumpets; 'tis always in the obscurity of a hidden corner, amid tears and sighing, that the new Evangel is born. It is never the superior classes, exactly because their position is too high, it is always the lower alone which are led on by the waves of the world's history."[2]

[1] Höffding, op. cit., p. 283.
[2] Postscript to the Introduction, second German edition of *The Essence of Christianity*.

He is important because he told us how long we human individuals endure, and why. He told us which of the supposedly God-given things in our world are chimerical or without significance, and which are eternal. He told us these things nearly a century ago. They are well recapitulated for our generation in a book called *The Bridge of San Luis Rey*:

"But soon we shall die. . . . We ourselves shall be loved for a while and forgotten. But the love will have been enough; all those impulses of love return to the love that made them. Even memory is not necessary for love. There is a land of the living and a land of the dead, and the bridge is love, the only survival, the only meaning."[1]

He is important because he told us that we ourselves have made our gods; that the emotions which we have thought were divine emotions are human emotions; that the lumps in our throats which we thought were transcendently produced are really produced by our own next-to-highest nature, our highest nature being the comprehension of our next-to-highest.

And he is important because he told us why we should turn away from the vanity of preoccupation with another world. This world is all. We have too long neglected to make it a better one, because we have thought ourselves to be but strangers here. We have been recreant in not turning our hands to the tasks which have been crying out to be done, not because we could not do them, but because we have been chasing a rainbow.

This is Feuerbach's contribution to history, to philo-

[1] Concluding reflections of the Abbess in Thornton Wilder's *The Bridge of San Luis Rey*.

sophy, and above all, to man. We are not naive enough to believe that the simple exposition of that contribution will work any miracles. Pedagogically speaking, Feuerbach was that naive; Marx, on the other hand, was not. To be more explicit, those who dwell in the camp of philosophical idealism will probably stay there even if they read Feuerbach, or Marx, incessantly and for decades. Materialism is not generally acceptable to them for reasons for which only materialism has an explanation. Only in so far as the whole *milieu* of the idealist changes, does his philosophy change. This book will not lead anyone to reject transcendent religion or personal immortality ideas by the force of its arguments; only as a concomitant of other, less abstract, influences will it work in that direction. It is addressed, then, to those to whom the major questions have already arisen, to those through whose minds has passed the cauterizing flame of socially-understood experience, or to those who have already moved into the area of thought in which this book dwells, but who have not achieved full self-clarification on some of the issues herein treated. To the extent to which this writing can be of even minor value to them, the labour expended in it has received far more than its socially-necessary reward.

We return to Feuerbach. His life was, by the standards of the world of business success, empty. His life was, by the standards of transcendent moralists and eschatologists, bitterly vain. But by the standards of genuine humanitarianism, by the standards of historical materialism, Feuerbach's life was as full and rich as that of any man of our era. He reaped neither earthly nor imaginary superearthly rewards. His immortality is in his species and in his work; of that immortality this book is a tiny part. He, and we, could crave no more.

It is often said that when a philosopher dies there is rejoicing both in heaven and on earth; in heaven, because he is rejoicing his comrades and colleagues, from Thales on down; and on earth, because he is no longer there to ask embarrassing questions. When Feuerbach died, there was no rejoicing in heaven, for it had ceased to exist; and on the earth there was no rejoicing, but only sorrow, because a good and great man had died.

*   *   *   *   *

Feuerbach was a philosopher. But philosophy to him was not an end in itself. "Erudition and philosophy are to me," he said, "only the *means* by which I bring to light the treasure hid in man." It is the knowledge of that treasure which makes all real things possible to us. To know that the unreal things are impossible is but the inverted form of that positive truth. For it we thank you, Ludwig Feuerbach.

Bibliography*

FEUERBACH:

Sämmtliche Werke, Leipzig, 1846–66.

Vol. I. *Erlauterungen und Erganzungen zum Wesen des Christenthums.*

Vol. II. *Philosophische Kritiken und Grundsätze.*

Vol. III. *Gedanken über Tod und Unsterblichkeit.*

Vol. IV. *Geschichte der neueren Philosophie von Bacon von Verulam bis Benedict Spinoza.*

Vol. V. *Darstellung, Entwicklung und Kritik der Leibnitz'schen Philosophie.*

Vol. VI. *Pierre Bayle, Ein Beitrag zur Geschichte der Philosophie und Menschheit.*

Vol. VII. *Das Wesen des Christenthums.*

Vol. VIII. *Vorlesungen über das Wesen der Religion.*

Vol. IX. *Theogonie nach den Quellen des klassischen hebraischen und christlichen Alterthums.*

Vol. X. *Gottheit, Freiheit und Unsterblichkeit vom Standpunkte der Anthropologie.*

Sämmtliche Werke, second edition; edited by Bolin and Jodl, Stuttgart, 1903–11.

The Essence of Christianity, translated from the second German edition by Marian Evans, London, 1853; (English translation of *Das Wesen des Christenthums*.)

Second edition, London, 1877.

* This bibliography contains works in German, French, and English. There is a further limited literature, not listed here, in Italian, Russian, and the Scandinavian languages.

La Réligion—Mort, Immortalité, Réligion, authorized French translation with commentary by Joseph Roy, Paris, 1864 (a compendium of Feuerbach's principal writings on immortality).

L'Essence de la Réligion, L'Essence du Christianisme, translated by A. H. Ewerbeck, Paris, 1850 (French translation of Feuerbach's principal writings on religion).

Ludwig Feuerbach in seinem Briefwechsel und Nachlass, edited by Karl Grün, 2 volumes, Leipzig and Heidelberg, 1874.

Ausgewählte Briefe, edited by Bolin, Leipzig, 1904.

Briefwechsel zwischen Feuerbach und C. Kapp, edited by A. Kapp, Leipzig, 1876.

Monographs and Critical Works:

C. BEYER: *Leben und Geist Feuerbach's,* 1873.

WILHELM BOLIN: *Ludwig Feuerbach: sein Wirken und seine Zeitgenossen,* Stuttgart, 1891.

FRIEDRICH ENGELS: *L. Feuerbach und der Ausgang der klassischen deutschen Philosophie,* Stuttgart, 1888 (English edition, London, 1934).

F. JODL: *Ludwig Feuerbach,* 1904.

A. KOHUT: *Ludwig Feuerbach; sein Leben und seine Werke,* 1909.

ALBERT LÉVY: *La Philosophie de Feuerbach et son Influence sur la Littérature Allemande,* Paris, 1904.

S. RAWIDOWICZ: *Ludwig Feuerbach's Philosophie—Ursprung und Schicksal,* Berlin, 1931.

CARL STARCKE: *Ludwig Feuerbach,* Stuttgart, 1885.

Miscellaneous Works dealing wholly or in part with Feuerbach:

J. A. CORNILL: *L. Feuerbach und seine Stellung zur Religion und Philosophie der Gegenwart*, 1851.

O. DOERING: *Feuerbachs Straftheorie und ihr Verhaltnis zur Kantischen Philosophie*, 1907.

H. DUENNEBIER: *Gottfried Keller und Ludwig Feuerbach*, 1913.

EPIGONI: *Die Triarier D. F. Strauss, L. Feuerbach, und A. Ruge*, 1852.

C. P. FISCHER: *Die Unwahrheit des Sensualismus und Materialismus*, 1853.

F. HARMS: *Der Anthropologismus . . . und L. Feuerbach's Anthroposophie*, 1845.

R. HAYM: *Feuerbach und die Philosophie*, 1847.

W. MACCALL: *The Newest Materialism*, 1873.

G. NUEDLING: *Ludwig Feuerbachs Religionsphilosophie*, 1936.

A. RAU: *L. Feuerbach's Philosophie*, 1882; *Harnack, Goethe, D. Strauss, und L. Feuerbach über das Wesen des Christenthums*, 1903.

REICHLIN-MELDEGG: *Die Autolatrie*, 1843.

A. RUGE: *Anekdota*, 1843.

E. A. VON SCHADEN: *Über den Gegensatz des theistischen und pantheistischen Standpunktes*, 1848.

J. SCHALLER: *Darstellung . . . der Philosophie L. Feuerbach's*, 1847.

C. SCHOLL: *Dem Andenken.*

Feuerbach and Marxism:

AUGUSTE CORNU: *Karl Marx, l'Homme et l'Œuvre*, Paris, 1934.

SIDNEY HOOK: *From Hegel to Marx*, London, 1936.

T. A. JACKSON: *Dialectics*, London, 1936.

MARX AND ENGELS: *Die Heilige Familie*, Frankfort, 1845.

MARX AND ENGELS: *Die Deutsche Ideologie*, Moscow, 1932 (published in English, London, 1938).

MEHRING: *Nachlass von Marx, Engels, und Lassalle*, Stuttgart, 1902.

A. THALHEIMER: *Introduction to Dialectical Materialism*, New York, 1936.

Index